# Investigating the Dhamma

# Investigating the Dhamma

## A Collection of Papers

by
Bhikkhu Bodhi

BPE
BPS Pariyatti Editions

BPS Pariyatti Editions
An imprint of Pariyatti Publishing
www.pariyatti.org



Published by Buddhist Publication Society, Kandy, Sri Lanka, 2015.

Published with the consent of the original publisher. Copies of this book for sale in the Americas only.

First BPS Pariyatti Edition, 2017
ISBN: 978-1-68172-068-5 (Print)
ISBN: 978-1-68172-071-5 (PDF)
ISBN: 978-1-68172-069-2 (ePub)
ISBN: 978-1-68172-070-8 (Mobi)
LCCN: 2017909194

Printed in the USA

# SOURCES

1. "Aggregates and Clinging Aggregates" was originally published in *Pali Buddhist Review*, Vol. 1, 1976, pp. 91–102. Reprinted with the permission of Russell Webb.
2. "Dance or Cessation?" is an unpublished paper written in 1989.
3. "Anattā as Strategy and Ontology" is an unpublished paper written in 1993.
4. "A Critical Examination of Ñāṇavīra's 'A Note on Paṭiccasamuppāda'" was originally published as two parts in *Buddhist Studies Review*. Vol. 15, No. 1, 1998: 43–64 and Vol. 15, No. 2, 1998: 157–181. Reprinted with the permission of Russell Webb.
5. "Review of *Buddhism without Beliefs*" was originally published in *Buddhist Publication Society Newsletter* No. 38, 1st Mailing 1998 and *Journal of Buddhist Ethics*, Vol. 5, 1998: 14–21.
6. "The Jhānas and the Lay Disciple" was originally published in *Buddhist Studies In Honour of Professor Lily de Silva*, edited by P.D. Premasiri et al, Peradeniya, 2001: 36–64. Reprinted with the permission of P.D. Premasiri.
7. "What Does Mindfulness Really Mean?" was originally published in *Contemporary Buddhism*, Vol. 12, 2011, pp. 19–39. Reprinted with the permission of Taylor & Francis Publishers.
8. "Deconstructing Constructions" is an unpublished paper written in 2014.

# Contents


Sources v
Contents vii
Preface ix
Abbreviations xi
Aggregates and Clinging Aggregates 1
Dance or Cessation? 15
1. Introduction 15
2. The Doctrine of Momentariness 16
3. The Wheel of Causation 17
4. The Unconditioned 18
5. The Concept of Freedom 20
6. The Problem of Escape 21
Anattā as Strategy and Ontology 25
1. Introduction 25
2. The Strategic Function of the Anattā-Teaching 27
3. The Anattā-Teaching Rests on an Ontology 29
4. The Ontology of the Conditioned 32
5. Why is the Anattā-teaching Effective? 35
6. The Right View of the Arahant 37
A Critical Examination of Ñāṇavīra Thera's "*A Note on Paṭiccasamuppāda*" 41
1. Introduction 41
2. Fundamental Attitudes 44
3. Birth, Aging and Death 48
4. Bhava and Rebirth 49
5. Three Types of Saṅkhārā 53
6. The Meaning of 'saṅkhārā' 57
7. Saṅkhārā in the PS Formula 59
8. In Defense of Tradition 68
9. The Problem of Time 72
10. The Knowledge of Final Deliverance 79
Review of Buddhism without Beliefs 83

THE JHĀNAS AND THE LAY DISCIPLE 91
1. Introduction 91
2. Jhāna and the Attainment of Stream-entry 95
3. Jhāna and Right Concentration 103
4. The Stream-enterer and Jhāna 106
5. When Do the Jhānas Become Necessary? 110
6. Conclusions and an Afterthought 116
WHAT DOES MINDFULNESS REALLY MEAN? 119
A Canonical Perspective 119
1. Mindfulness in the Buddhist Path 119
2. The Meaning of 'sati' 122
3. Mindfulness and Bare Attention 129
4. What the Suttas Say 137
5. Clear Comprehension 139
6. Expanding into New Frontiers 141
BIBLIOGRAPHY 144
DECONSTRUCTING CONSTRUCTIONS: 145
1. Introduction 145
2. Saṅkhārā in Dependent Origination 146
3. Saṅkhārā as the Fourth Aggregate 150
4. Saṅkhārā as All Conditioned Things 152
5. The Sequential Cessation of Saṅkhārā 156
6. A Synoptic Perspective on the Saṅkhārā 158
7. Deconstructing Constructions 160

# PREFACE

This book brings together eight essays of Venerable Bhikkhu Bodhi, five of which have been published in academic journals, and three of which have not been published before. The aim of this collection is to make these essays available to a wider readership as well as to celebrate Bhikkhu Bodhi's seventieth birthday.

Most of the essays are critiques of modern interpretations or reinterpretations of aspects of the Dhamma that Bhikkhu Bodhi considers to be at odds with the Buddha's teachings. These responses are made from the perspective of a traditional Theravāda scholar and practitioner who has an academic background in Western philosophy and therefore are of interest to both practicing Buddhists and academics.

The essays show Bhikkhu Bodhi's great knowledge of the Dhamma as well as his unwavering dedication in promoting a right understanding of it. While *Dhamma Reflections*, the previous collection of essays by Bhikkhu Bodhi published by BPS, mainly contained short essays written for a wider Buddhist readership, the essays in the present book deal with profound aspects of the Dhamma and mostly were written for those who are more familiar with the Buddha's teachings of the Theravāda tradition.

The essays are arranged in chronological order, starting with an essay written in 1976 and finishing with an essay written in 2014. Here is a brief overview of the essays:

*Essay 1*, "Aggregates and Clinging Aggregates" is a detailed investigation of the meaning of the five aggregates of clinging (*pañcupādānakkhandhā*).

*Essay 2*, "Dance or Cessation?" is a refutation of the unorthodox views of the eco-philosopher Joanna Macy regarding nibbāna, dependent arising, and the idea of momentariness.

*Essay 3*, "Anattā as Strategy and Ontology" is a critique of Ajahn Ṭhānissaro's "Not-self strategy," arguing that the Buddha's anattā-teaching is both pragmatic and ontological.

*Essay 4*, "A Critical Examination of Ñāṇavīra's 'A Note on Paṭiccasamuppāda'" is a critique of the "one-life interpretation" of the twelve-factored formula of dependent arising. Bhikkhu

Bodhi shows that some of the Buddha's discourses do support the traditional three-lives interpretation.

*Essay 5*, "Review of *Buddhism without Beliefs*" reviews a book of the agnostic Buddhist writer Stephen Batchelor. Bhikkhu Bodhi questions the author's idea that the Buddha's teaching should be viewed as "an existential, therapeutic, and liberating agnosticism."

*Essay 6*, "The Jhānas and the Lay Disciple" is an investigation of whether the jhānas are necessary for the attainment of the first stage of awakening, known as stream-entry.

*Essay 7*, "What Does Mindfulness Really Mean?" examines the original meaning of *sati*, "mindfulness" in the Buddha's teachings in contrast to modern popular therapeutic interpretations.

*Essay 8*, "Deconstructing Constructions" explores the Pāli term *saṅkhārā*, one of the pivotal concepts in the Buddha's discourses.

The abbreviation and reference system of Pāli texts that was used in the earlier essays has been adapted to fit the modern system as used in the later essays. Moreover, the sections of the earlier essays have been numbered in the manner of the later essays. Section headings have been added to the third essay to make it more accessible.

BPS Editor

# Abbreviations

Unless marked otherwise, all references to Pāli texts are to the editions published by the Pali Text Society. Canonical references are to sutta number, followed by volume and page of the Pali Text Society Pāli edition. In essay 7 these are in turn followed by title and page number of the translations of the "Teachings of the Buddha" Series of Wisdom Publications.

| | |
|---|---|
| A | Aṅguttara Nikāya (PTS page number) |
| AN | Aṅguttara Nikāya (Sutta number) |
| As | *Atthasālinī*, *Dhammasaṅgaṇī-aṭṭhakathā* |
| CDB | *Connected Discourses of the Buddha* (Bhikkhu Bodhi, Boston 2000) |
| D | Dīgha Nikāya (PTS page number) |
| DN | Dīgha Nikāya (Sutta number) |
| LDB | *Long Discourses of the Buddha* (Maurice Walshe, Boston 1995) |
| MLDB | *Middle Length Discourses of the Buddha* (Ñāṇamoli and Bodhi, Boston 1995) |
| M | Majjhima Nikāya (PTS page number) |
| MN | Majjhima Nikāya (Sutta number) |
| Mp | *Manorathapuraṇī*, *Aṅguttara-nikāya-aṭṭhakathā* |
| NDB | *The Numerical Discourses of the Buddha* (Bhikkhu Bodhi, Boston 2012) |
| Paṭis | Paṭisambhidāmagga |
| Pp | Puggalapaññatti |
| PTS | Pali Text Society |
| SĀ | Saṃyuktāgama |
| S | Saṃyutta Nikāya (PTS page number) |
| SN | Saṃyutta Nikāya (Sutta number) |
| Sn | Suttanipāta (Verse number) |
| Spk | *Sāratthapakkāsinī*, *Saṃyutta-nikāya-aṭṭhakathā* |
| T | Taishō Chinese Tripiṭaka (CBETA edition) |
| Vism | *Visuddhimagga* |

# Aggregates and Clinging Aggregates

## (*Khandhā/Upādānakkhandhā*)

### Part I

The Buddha's Teaching is concerned with a single problem, the problem of *dukkha* or suffering, and the task it imposes is likewise of a single nature—the task, namely, of bringing *dukkha* to an end.

In the standard formulation of the Four Noble Truths, the Buddha defines the truth of dukkha, the first Noble Truth, thus:

> "What, monks, is the Noble Truth of Dukkha? Birth is dukkha, decay is dukkha, death is dukkha, sorrow, lamentation, pain, displeasure and despair are dukkha; union with the unpleasant is dukkha, separation from the pleasant is dukkha, not to get what one wants is dukkha; in brief, the five aggregates of clinging are dukkha. This, monks, is the Noble Truth of Dukkha." (DN 22)

The five aggregates of clinging (*pañcupādānakkhandhā*) present a complete epitome of *dukkha*, both extensively by way of range and intensively by way of essence. Since this is so, we sometimes find that the formula for the first truth deletes the specific instances of *dukkha* and defines its subject matter directly as the aggregates:

> "What, monks, is the Noble Truth of Dukkha? The answer is: the five aggregates of clinging; that is, the clinging aggregate of material form, the clinging aggregate of feeling, the clinging aggregate of perception, the clinging aggregate of volitional determinations, and the clinging aggregate of consciousness. This, monks, is the Noble Truth of Dukkha."[1]

---

1. SN 56:13/S V 425: *Katamañ ca bhikkhave dukkhaṃ ariyasaccaṃ? Pañcupā-dānakkhandhā ti'ssa vacanīyaṃ, seyyathidaṃ rūpupādānakkhandho vedanupādā-nakkhandho saññupādānakkhandho saṅkhārūpādānakkhandho viññāṇupādā-nakkhandho. Idaṃ vuccati bhikkhave dukkhaṃ ariyasaccaṃ.*

The five clinging aggregates, in their assemblage, constitute *sakkāya*, the "existing body" or empirical personality. Therefore, on the grounds that things, i.e. personality and dukkha, equal to the same thing, i.e. the five clinging aggregates, are equal to each other, the structural formula of the four truths is occasionally stated in terms of *sakkāya* rather than dukkha (e.g. MN 44). Again, since all the five aggregates arise in connection with each of the six internal sense bases—the visual, auditory, olfactory, gustatory, tactile, and conceptual bases—the Noble Truth of Suffering may be explained as the six internal bases (*cha ajjhattikāni āyatanāni*, SN 56:14/S V 426).

In order to reach a proper understanding of the Buddha's Teaching, it is necessary to discover exactly what is meant by the five aggregates of clinging. For these are, as we see, dukkha, and it is just dukkha and the cessation of dukkha that the Buddha teaches. But our concern here is not to spell out in detail the content of each aggregate. That can readily be gleaned from the suttas, especially the Khandhasaṃyutta of the Saṃyuttanikāya. Our concern, rather, is to determine what precisely is intended by calling the aggregates "the five clinging aggregates," and to see what implications this has for our understanding of dukkha. While such an investigation may appear initially as a trifling enterprise, just one more instance of scholastic hair-splitting raising an unnecessary cloud of dust, further thought will show that, to the contrary, an exact determination of the meaning of the term *pañcupādānakkhandhā* is of prime importance in arriving at a correct grasp of the Dhamma. For it is these aggregates, as the categories of dukkha, that provide the Dhamma with its irreplaceable point of departure, and their remainderless fading away and cessation that stands as its final consummation.

The take-off point for any inquiry into the significance of the term "clinging aggregates" will naturally be the import of the qualifying attribute "clinging" (*upādāna*). The word *upādāna*, an intensification of the noun *ādāna*, "taking," indicates a mental attitude of firm grasping or holding (*daḷhagahaṇa*). When used as a prefix to form the compound term *upādānakkhandha*, it might first be taken to imply that each aggregate is a *form of clinging*, and hence that the five clinging aggregates are the aggregates which are modalities or activities of clinging. But an analytical breakdown of *upādāna* shows that not all the aggregates are forms of clinging, but only two components of the *saṅkhārakkhandha*, the aggregate of volitional determinations or mental formations. According to the *suttas* (MN 9) there are four types of clinging: clinging to sense-pleasures (*kāmupādāna*), clinging to wrong views (*diṭṭhupādāna*), clinging to rules and observances (*sīlabbatupādāna*), and clinging to a belief in self (*attavādupādāna*). The first is a mode of the mental factor of greed (*lobha*), the latter three of the mental factor of wrong views (*diṭṭhi*).[2] Both these mental factors belong exclusively to the *saṅkhārakkhandha*. Hence to regard the aggregates as five forms of clinging cannot be correct.

As a second alternative, one might take the compound term "clinging aggregates" to mean "aggregates which are the abode of clinging." In such a case one would then go on to identify the clinging aggregates with the aggregates of the non-arahat, in whom clinging in some form and to some degree is always present, at least dormantly, while the aggregates of the arahat would become bare aggregates but not clinging aggregates, since the arahat has extinguished all clinging. Such a move would imply that the range of dukkha is to be circumscribed by the experience of the non-arahat, and the experience of the arahat to be left fully exempt from the category of dukkha. This interpretation has, at first glance, a presumptive plausibility, especially if dukkha is understood in the sense of experiential suffering; for the arahat, the suttas leave no doubt, has gone beyond the possibility of any experience of suffering except bare bodily pain, and even that arouses in him not antipathy. Nevertheless, this interpretation too is not correct. But before going on to examine the issue at a deeper level, let us first fix our definitions of terms.

The only sutta to our knowledge where two sets of aggregates are explicitly defined, (*not* contrasted, it should be observed), is the Khandha Sutta. The definitions of the two sets, in a condensed translation, are as follows:

(1) The five aggregates (*pañcakkhandhā*):

> "What, monks, are the five aggregates? Whatever material form, feeling, perception, volitional determinations, consciousness there may be—past, present, or future, internal or external, coarse or subtle, inferior or superior, far or near—these are the aggregates of material form, feeling, perception, volitional

2. Dhammasaṅgaṇī (Dhs) §§ 1219–1223 (Chaṭṭhasaṅgāyana ed.).

determinations, and consciousness. These, monks, are the five aggregates."

(2) The five clinging aggregates (*pañcupādānakkhandhā*):

> "And what, monks, are the five clinging-aggregates? Whatever material form, feeling, perception, volitional determinations, consciousness there may be—past, present, or future, internal or external, coarse or subtle, inferior or superior, far or near, that are subject to the cankers, subject to clinging (*sāsavaṃ upādāniyaṃ*)—these are the clinging aggregates of material form, feeling, perception, volitional determinations, and consciousness. These, monks, are the five clinging aggregates."[3]

Now because the five clinging aggregates are each individually instances of material form, feeling, perception, volitional determinations, and consciousness, they are each individually included *in toto* among the five aggregates, in their respective categories; that is, any material form comprised in the clinging aggregate of material form will necessarily also belong to the aggregate of material form, and so with the rest. But the fact that a differentiation is drawn between the two sets with the phrase *sāsava upādāniya* implies that a genuine difference in range does exist: that there are, in other words, aggregates of each sort which are *anāsava anupādāniya.* These we may call "the bare five aggregates," though we will see shortly that this phrase must be qualified in one respect. The question is then: what are these bare five aggregates? One might be tempted, in line with the interpretation sketched above, to equate the bare five aggregates with the arahat's aggregates in all his experience. But this is an equation which does not find support in a single sutta, and, moreover, even appears to be negated by at least one sutta passage, repeated in two consecutive suttas by the venerable Sāriputta:

3. SN 22:48/S III 47: *Katame ca bhikkhave pañcakkhandhā? Yaṃ kiñci bhikkhave rūpaṃ ... viññāṇaṃ atītānāgatapaccuppannaṃ ajjhattaṃ vā bahiddhā vā olārikaṃ vā sukhumaṃ vā hīnaṃ vā paṇītaṃ vā yaṃ dūre santike vā, ayaṃ vuccati rūpakkhandho (... viññāṇakkhandho). Ime vuccanti bhikkhave pañcakkha-ndhā. Katame ca bhikkhave pañcupādānakkhandhā? Yaṃ kiñci bhikkhave rūpaṃ ... viññāṇaṃ atītānāgata-paccuppannaṃ ... yaṃ dūre santike vā sāsavaṃ upādāniyaṃ, ayaṃ vuccati rūpupādānakkhandho ... viññāṇūpādānakkhandho. Ime vuccanti bhikkhave pañcupādānakkhandhā.*

"Even the arahat, friend Koṭṭhita, should wisely consider the five clinging aggregates as impermanent, suffering, a disease, a boil, a dart, a flaw, an affliction, as alien, disintegrating, empty, and not-self. For the arahat who has completed his task there is no higher achievement. But these practices, cultivated and developed, conduce to his pleasant abiding in the present state and to mindfulness and clear comprehension."[4]

Thus the arahat, this text implies, is also composed of the five clinging aggregates. In what sense this is true we will soon see. Here we should note that the "pleasant abiding" referred to is not mundane *jhāna*, for that does not require prior insight work on the aggregates; nor is it the attainment of cessation (*nirodha-samāpatti*), for that cannot be achieved by every arahat whereas the text gives a general prescription. It is, rather, the special attainment, accessible only to the arahat, called the *arahattapha-lasamāpatti*, the attainment of the fruit of arahatship, in which the world disappears and Nibbāna remains, yielding the arahat the experience of the bliss of emancipation, the taste of the deathless, even in the midst of this mortal world. And it is in this attainment, we will see, as well as in the other supramundane states of consciousness, that the clinging aggregates cease and the bare aggregates alone stand.

In order to discover the denotations of the two terms "the five clinging aggregates" and "the bare five aggregates" we must first determine the exact meanings of the two terms that distinguish them, *sāsava* and *upādāniya*. The latter term is used in the suttas in connection with the aggregates to mean "subject to clinging," in the sense that the things they denote are capable of being taken as the objects of clinging or *upādāna*. For example, the *Upādāniya Sutta* says: "Material form, ... feeling, ... perception, ... volitional determinations, ... consciousness, monks is a state subject to clinging. The desire-and-lust for that, that is the clinging to it."[5] The

4. SN 22:122/S III 168: *Arahatā pi kho āvuso Koṭṭhita ime pañcupādānakkhandhā, aniccato dukkhato rogato gaṇḍato sallato aghato ābādhato parato palokato suññato anattato yoniso manasikātabbā. Natthi khvāvuso arahato uttari karaṇīyaṃ, katassa vā paticayo. Api ca ime dhammā bhāvitā bahulikatā diṭṭhadha-m-masukhavihārāya c'eva saṃvattanti satisampajaññāya ca.*

5. SN 22:121/S III 167: *Rūpaṃ, ...vedanā, ... saññā, ... saṅkhārā, ... viññāṇaṃ upādāniyo dhammo, yo tattha chandarāgo taṃ tattha upādānaṃ.*

word *sāsava* is not, to our knowledge, used specifically in relation to the five aggregates in the suttas, except in the Khandha Sutta, but one may assume it to be the equivalent to *upādāniya* in terms of the *āsavas* or cankers; that is, to denote things capable of being taken as the objects of the *āsavas.* This assumption is borne out by the commentary to the above sutta. The commentary says: "*Sāsava:* a condition for the cankers as an object. *Upādāniya*: a condition of the same type for the clingings. The meaning of the term *sāsava* is a state occurring in conjunction with the cankers which take it as their object."[6]

To find an exact and detailed breakdown of the two groups, *sāsava dhamma* and *upādāniya dhamma*, we must turn to the first book of the Abhidhammapiṭaka, the Dhammasaṅgaṇī, which sets itself the special task of fully spelling out in terms of ultimate, actually existent states, the precise denotations of such technically significant expressions. According to the Dhammasaṅgaṇī (§ 594), all material form (*rūpa*) is *sāsava* and *upādāniya*, since all material form may become the object of the cankers and clingings. Thus the contents of the aggregate of form (*rūpakkhandha*) and the clinging aggregate of form (*rūpupādānakkhandha*) completely coincide. There is no bare aggregate of material form. When, henceforth, we speak of a "bare five aggregates," it is only figurative, for there at most four aggregates which are *anāsava* and *anupādāniya.* But more important, according to the same work (§ 1108, 1225, 1467, 1555), the immaterial aggregates of the arahat which are resultant (*vipāka*) as well as active (*kiriya*) in the mundane sphere, either sensuous or jhānic, are also *sāsava* and *upādāniya*. This is so not in the sense that they are still pregnant with the cankers and clinging, for it is plain that all defilements are abandoned by the arahat, but in the sense that they can become the objects of the defilements of others. Any feeling, perception, volitional determination, or consciousness, internal or external (*ajjhattaṃ vā bahiddhā vā*), that can become the object of the cankers and clinging is *sāsava upādāniya.* And further, since all *sāsava upādāniya* aggregates are

6. Spk II 270: *Sāsavan ti āsavānaṃ ārammaṇabhāvena paccayabhūtaṃ. Upādāniyan ti tatheva ca upādānānaṃ paccayabhūtaṃ. Vacanattho panettha ārammaṇaṃ katvā pavattehi saha āsavehīti sāsavaṃ. Upādātabban ti upādāniyaṃ.*

clinging aggregates (*upādānakkhandha*), this means that the arahat's mundane experience is still five clinging aggregates, though of course no clinging will be found therein. There is actually no such thing as "one's own aggregates" or "the aggregates of others," differently classifiable according to the perspective. There are only aggregates internal and external, and all aggregates internal or external that can become objects of the cankers and clingings are to be classified as the five clinging aggregates. The bare aggregates, then, will be those aggregates which cannot become objects of the defilements either internally or externally. And what are those aggregates? They are, in the classification of the Dhammasaṅgaṇī (§ 1109, 1226, 1468, 1556), the immaterial aggregates—feeling, perception, volitional determinations, and consciousness—of the supramundane states of consciousness, the ariyan paths and fruits; for these states of consciousness cannot be apprehended by a mind defiled with the *āsavas* and *upādāna* due to their sublime purity, a purity flowing from the absolute purity of their object, Nibbāna.

This point is not made explicitly in the suttas, but it is implied by a number of passages (MN 22, AN 9:9/A V 324, etc.) showing the inability of the gods to discern the consciousness of the arahat when he is in the *phalasamāpatti*, as also by the texts urging the arahat to contemplate the unsatisfactoriness of the five clinging aggregates in order to withdraw from them and "abide pleasantly in this present state." In the *Atthasālinī*, however, the commentary to the Dhammasaṅgaṇī, the issue is directly confronted. In order to explain why the Abhidhamma text classifies the mundane aggregates of the arahat as *upādāniya* and the aggregates of the noble paths, fruits, and Nibbāna as alone *anupādāniya*, the commentator writes: "Although the aggregates of the arahat who has destroyed the cankers become conditions for clinging in others, when they say, for example, 'Our senior uncle the Thera! Our junior uncle the Thera!,' the noble paths, fruits, and Nibbāna are not grasped, misapprehended, or clung to. Just as a red-hot iron ball does not provide a resting-place for flies to settle, so the noble paths, fruits, and Nibbāna, due to their abundant spiritual sublimity, do not provide a condition for grasping through craving, conceit, and wrong views."[7]

---

7. As 347: *Upādiṇṇattike kiñcāpi khīṇāsavassa khandhā 'amhākaṃ mātulatthero amhākaṃ cūḷapitutthero'ti vadantānaṃ paresaṃ upādānassa*

Thus the mundane aggregates of the arahat, no less than those of a worldling, pertain to the five clinging aggregates. The five aggregates will include all states, those subject to clinging and those not subject to clinging; the five clinging aggregates will include only those subject to clinging, i.e. the potential objects of clinging; and the "bare aggregates" will refer to the immaterial aggregates of the supramundane paths and fruits which elude the grasp of clinging.

It may be objected that our conclusion drawn from the Dhammasaṅgaṇī is contradicted by the Cūḷavedalla Sutta (MN 44), where we read in the Pali: *Yo kho āvuso Visākha pañcupādānakkhandhesu chandarāgo taṃ tattha upādānaṃ.* This text one might be tempted to translate: "The desire-and-lust that is in the five clinging aggregates, that is the clinging therein." Such a translation, however, is quite incorrect and leads to a wrong construction of the meaning of the passage and consequently of the concept of *dukkha.* In Pali grammar the objects of desire are generally set in the locative case—whether nominal or pronominal—and this principle is exemplified in the above statement. It is not the desire-and-lust contained *within* the five clinging aggregates that is the clinging *therein*, (though clinging will surely be present at least incipiently in all non-arahats). Rather, it is the desire-and-lust *for* the five clinging aggregates that is the clinging *to* them. The Upādāniya Sutta cited above should be recalled, where it is said: "Material form ... consciousness is an *upādāniya dhamma*," and *yo tattha chandarāgo taṃ tattha upādānaṃ*, "the desire-and-lust for that, that is the clinging to it." Clinging is not contained within the form, feeling, perception, and consciousness aggregates, but only within part of the aggregate of volitional determinations, the *saṅkhārakkhandha.* But the desire-and-lust *for* form, *for* feeling, *for* perception, *for* the volitions, *for* consciousness, that is the clinging *to* them. And each aggregate is itemized separately in relation to clinging, leaving no suspicion that a collective meaning ("the clinging within the set of five") might be intended. Other suttas teach the same lesson with regard to other categories of states, as for example: *Cakkhuṃ, bhikkhave, upādāniyo dhammo, yo*

---

*paccayā honti, maggaphalanibbānāni pana aggahitāni aparāmaṭṭhāni anupādiṇṇāneva. Tāni hi, yathā divasaṃ santatto ayoguḷo makkhikānaṃ abhinisīdanassa paccayo na hoti, evameva tejussadattā taṇhāmānadiṭṭhivasena gahaṇassa paccayā na honti.*

*tattha chandarāgo taṃ tattha upādānaṃ:* "The eye, monks, is a state subject to clinging; the desire-and-lust for that, that is the clinging to it" (SN 35:110/S IV 89). Again, desire-and-lust, or clinging, is certainly not contained within the eye, but takes the eye as its object; and so with the remaining sense-faculties and their objects. In the same way, clinging is not necessarily contained within the five clinging aggregates, (though it very well may be), but it takes the five clinging aggregates, either internally or externally, as its object. The meaning of the phrase "there is no clinging apart from the five clinging aggregates" (*na pi aññatara pañcupādānakkhandhesu upādānaṃ*) is that there is no clinging that does not have the clinging aggregates as its objective reference.

Whatever can be clung to is classified within the five aggregates of clinging. Thence there is no contradiction between the designation of the arahat as five clinging aggregates and the recognition of his freedom from clinging: the term "five clinging aggregates" denotes the aggregates that provide the objective range for clinging, not the aggregates that contain clinging.[8]

## PART II

The conclusion reached above—that the five clinging aggregates are to be construed as the potential objects of clinging rather than as the abode of clinging—paves the way to a correct understanding of the statement of the first Noble Truth: "in brief, the five aggregates of clinging are *dukkha.*" The Four Noble Truths are formulated with a specific purpose in view. They are taught as a practical and deliberate course of instruction designed to lead onward, by the very pattern of their arrangement, to the achievement of a particular end. The end they are designed to lead to is the end of the Buddha's Dispensation itself—disenchantment, detachment, cessation, peace, comprehension, enlightenment, and Nibbāna.[9] Now, the primary

8. See Vism XIV.215: "Aggregates that are the resort of clinging are aggregates of clinging" (*upādānagocarā khandha upādānakkhandhā*), translation by Bhikkhu Ñāṇamoli, *The Path of Purification*, (Kandy, 1975), p. 543.

9. See e.g., MN 63/M I 431: '*Idaṃ dukkhan'ti.... 'ayaṃ dukkhanirodhagāminī paṭipadā'ti. ... etaṃ ... nibbidāya virāgāya nirodhāya upasamāya abhiññāya sambodhāya nibbānāya saṃvattati.*

impediment to the realization of Nibbāna is craving (*taṇhā*). In the metaphorical language of the suttas, craving is the seamstress that binds the evolving consciousness to the round of repeated existence, obstructing the entrance to the courseway to liberation. To reach deliverance, therefore, craving must be abandoned. When craving intensifies, it turns into clinging (*upādāna*), which springs up and thrives upon an objective field provocative of clinging. This objective field, potentially identical with the mundane world in its totality, can be classified for pedagogical purposes into five basic categories, namely, the five aggregates of clinging. To remove clinging, and its underlying root, craving, the mind must be made to turn away from the objective field of clinging. Such an inward revulsion can only come about when the objective field of clinging, always beckoning with the lure of gratification, is seen in true perspective, as essentially suffering. Thence the Buddha's reduction of the mundane world to the five aggregates of clinging, and the equation of the aggregates themselves with dukkha.

The Buddha's aim, then, in formulating the first Noble Truth in the way stated is to lead people to deliverance by getting them to put away craving for all things capable of arousing craving, that is, for the five aggregates. The *puthujjanā*, the common people of the world, are impelled by their desire and false thinking to perceive pleasurableness in the aggregates, internal and external. Thence, with their perception, thought, and outlook twisted by the perverse apprehension of pleasure in what is truly suffering, they relish the aggregates and cling to them with desire-and-lust. Through their clinging they generate a chain of *kammic formations* that fetters them to the round of repeated births, and entering into birth they reap all the suffering consequent upon birth.

> "When one dwells, contemplating gratification in things subject to clinging (*upādāniyesu dhammesu assādānupassino viharato*), craving increases; conditioned by craving, clinging comes to be; conditioned by clinging, existence; conditioned by existence, birth; conditioned by birth, decay and death, sorrow, lamentation, pain, displeasure, and despair come to be. Such is the origination of this entire mass of suffering. It is just as if, monks, a great mass of fire were to be blazing upon ten, twenty, thirty, or forty loads of fire-wood, and a man were from time

to time to throw upon it dry grass, cowdung, and logs. That great mass of fire, with such nutriment, with such a stock of fuel, would continue blazing for a long, long time." (SN 12:52/S II 84)

In order to help the common people get free from this mass of suffering, the Buddha must induce them to give up their desire for the objects provocative of desire with which they are enthralled; for it is this desire—craving nourished by ignorance—that turns the wheel of the round. To get people to give up desire, the Buddha points out that the things they take to be pleasurable, i.e. the five clinging aggregates, are really unpleasurable, dukkha, when seen with right understanding as they really are—as impermanent, insecure, perilous, masterless, coreless, and egoless. Whatever can be seized upon with desire as pleasurable must now be contemplated with insight (*vipassanā*) as unpleasurable. Thus the five aggregates which are the range of clinging are also defined, implicitly in the suttas and explicitly in the commentaries, as the aggregates which are the soil of insight.[10] When the people to be guided hear the Dhamma, acquire faith, undertake the training, develop insight, and reach the noble path, they see with right view for themselves that all the objects of desire, potential and actual, are dukkha. Equipped with this right view, they are able to cut through their confusion, extinguish the fire of craving, and achieve deliverance from birth-and-death.

> "But when, monks, one dwells contemplating the unsatisfactoriness in things subject to clinging (*upādānīyesu dhammesu ādīnavānupassino viharato*), craving ceases. With the cessation of craving, clinging ceases, with the cessation of clinging, existence, ... birth, ... decay and death, sorrow, lamentation, pain, displeasure, and despair cease. Such is the cessation of this entire mass of suffering. It is just as if, monks, a great mass of fire were to be blazing upon ten, twenty, thirty, or forty loads, of firewood, and nobody would throw dry grass, cowdung,

10. "The states subject to the cankers are designated the 'clinging aggregates' for the purpose of pointing out the soil of insight" (*vipassanābhū-misandassanatthaṃ pana sāsavā vā upādānakkhandhā ti*). *Abhidhammatthasaṅgaha*, p. 229 (Chaṭṭhasaṅgāyana ed.).

> and logs, upon it from time to time. That great mass of fire, due to the exhaustion of its original stock of fuel and the non-acquisition of any more fuel, devoid of nutriment, would be extinguished." (SN 12:52/S II 85)

Now, because the arahat's mundane aggregates can be made into objects of desire-and-lust, they too enter into the five aggregates of clinging. They cannot be clung to by the arahat himself, for in the arahat all clinging has been uprooted, made of a nature never to arise again. But they can be clung to and evoke clinging in others. Only the immaterial aggregates of the supramundane states of consciousness, the ariyan paths and fruits, together with Nibbāna, cannot be taken as objects by the defilements: these, therefore, alone constitute the "bare aggregates." The arahat's aggregates in his mundane experience, however, are still five clinging aggregates. They are still *sakkāya* and still *dukkha*. They can no longer cause any mental sorrow or suffering in the arahat, for they are totally devoid of any subjective significance for him. But they remain dukkha for others in the sense that they can lead to suffering when held to with desire-and-lust, and for the arahat in the deeper sense that they are felt as inherently unsatisfactory compared to their temporary cessation in the *phalasamāpatti*, when the arahat experiences the bliss of Nibbāna, and compared especially to their final cessation in the *anupādisesanibbānadhātu*, the Nibbāna-element without residue, when the aggregates will cease, never to arise again.

Thus the arahat understands that all the disturbances due to the *āsavas* have finally ceased for him; but a measure of disturbance (*darathamatta*), subjectively indifferent, continues, dependent only on the body with its six sense-faculties which remain intact until the end of his life-span (MN 121/M III 108). So long as the arahat remains alive, so long his sense- faculties operate and so long he experiences, by means of his sense-faculties, feelings that are pleasant, painful and neutral. But "whatever is felt, that is included in dukkha."[11] The feelings are impermanent, and "whatever is impermanent is dukkha" (SN 12:32/S II 53). The great arahat disciple Sāriputta compares the oppression he feels from his own body to the oppression of snakes and corpses, and the maintenance of his body

11. MN 136/M III 208, SN 12:32/S II 53, SN 36:11/S IV 216: *Yaṃ kiñci vedayitaṃ taṃ dukkhasmin ti.*

to that of fatty excrescences (AN 9:11/A IV 376). And the Vibhaṅga of the Abhidhammapiṭaka (Vibh IV.2, § 190/p. 98), in confirmation of our conclusion that the arahat's experience is still *dukkha*, incorporates the resultant (*vipāka*) and functional (*kiriya*) aggregates which comprise the totality of the arahat's mundane experience in each one of its diverse expositions of the *dukkhasacca*. Thence when the arahat does pass finally away, one with right view understands: "Material form, feeling, perception, volitional determinations, and consciousness are impermanent. What is impermanent is dukkha. It is dukkha that has ceased, *dukkha* that has come to an end."[12] And the Buddha himself certifies the *parinibbāna* of the arahat disciples with the words: "He cut off craving, severed the fetters, and by fully penetrating conceit, he has made an end to dukkha."[13]

The fact that the arahat's mundane experience is also to be comprised within the range of dukkha implies that the term *dukkha* has a deeper, more difficult to grasp meaning than is suspected even by those who have overcome the hurdle of identifying dukkha with experienced suffering. The word *dukkha* seems to be used in four distinct yet intertwined senses in the suttas. In one sense it is physical pain, or painful feeling arisen through bodily contact, and as such is contrasted with *domanassa*, mental pain, or painful feeling arisen through mind contact. In a second sense *dukkha* embraces all unpleasant feeling, both physical and mental, *dukkha* and *domanassa*, as well as the broader experiences these feelings dominate—sorrow, lamentation, pain, grief, despair, etc. These first two senses together constitute *dukkha-dukkhatā* or experiential suffering. In a third sense *dukkha* indicates whatever is capable of issuing in suffering; that is, various things and experiences which, though pleasurable in their immediacy, may lead to suffering as their consequence, when they change or become otherwise. This is the meaning of *vipariṇāma-dukkhatā*, suffering due to change, which signifies not the suffering following upon change (this is already included under *dukkha-dukkhatā*), but the pleasurable experience itself, in its concrete immediacy, as a potential source of suffering. The fourth—the deep-

12. SN 22:85/S III 112: ... *viññāṇaṃ aniccaṃ. Yadaniccaṃ taṃ dukkhaṃ; yaṃ dukkhaṃ taṃ niruddhaṃ tadatthaṅgatan ti.*

13. SN 36:3/S IV 205: ... *acchecchi taṇhaṃ, vivattayi saṃyojanaṃ, sammā mānābhisamayā antamakāsi dukkhassā ti.*

est and most philosophical meaning of *dukkha*, completely divorced from any overtone of felt suffering whether actual or potential—is dukkha as inherent unsatisfactoriness. This is the *saṅkhāra-dukkhatā*, the dukkha that inheres in all the conditioned phenomena of mundane existence. This aspect of dukkha takes in all phenomena included in the three planes of becoming; it lays claim to the experience of the arahat no less than that of the worldling. Dukkha in this last sense is a philosophical, not a psychological, category. It is a world-embracing thought, the ultimate pronouncement made on the world of conditioned experience by one who has escaped from the world and gained access to the unconditioned. It is this meaning of dukkha that is intended by such statements as "all formations are dukkha," "whatever is impermanent is dukkha," "whatever is felt is included in dukkha," and by the statement of the first Noble Truth: "in brief, the five aggregates of clinging are dukkha." Dukkha here derives its significance entirely from its contrast with what is not conditionally produced, not impermanent, not subject to arising and passing away, i.e. with Nibbāna, the unconditioned element. That is why it is only the ariyan disciple who has seen Nibbāna for himself with the eye of noble wisdom, who can understand through direct penetration this last meaning of dukkha. For he alone has accessible to his vision a reality transcendent to the aggregates that are dukkha with which he can contrast them and see for himself that "in brief, the five aggregates of clinging are dukkha."

# Dance or Cessation?

*A Theravadin Reply to*
*"The Third Turning of the Wheel"*

## 1. Introduction

I would like to offer some comments, from a traditional Theravadin perspective, on "The Third Turning of the Wheel," the interview with Joanna Macy that was published in the Winter 1989 issue of *Inquiring Mind*.[14] If Joanna had restricted herself simply to proposing a new interpretation of Buddhism which she believes is better suited to our age than the classical version, then I would have been content to remain silent. But what particularly troubles me and moves me to write is the claim she puts forth repeatedly in the interview that the Theravada tradition has seriously misinterpreted some of the most important of the Buddha's original teachings. This conclusion, I feel, arises out of a cluster of factual and textual misunderstandings that call out for correction, especially so because Joanna attempts to support her position by allusion to and citations from the Pali suttas.

My discussion will be framed around Joanna's statement that "in the later Abhidharma texts of the Theravada, three fundamental shifts occurred that many people erroneously assign to the Buddha himself," namely: (1) the classification of nibbāna as an unconditioned dhamma; (2) the interpretation of the wheel of causation as a chronological sequence of three lives; and (3) the idea of momentariness, where the dhammas occur so rapidly that they do not last long enough to affect each other.

---

14. Republished in *Dharma Rain: Sources of Buddhist Environmentalism*, edited by S. Kaza & K. Kraft, Boston, 2000, pp. 150–160. (Viewable on books.google.com). Republished in abridged form in *The Best of Inquiring Mind: 25 Years of Dharma, Drama, and Uncommon Insight*, edited by B. Gates & W. Nisker, Boston 2008, pp. 277–280.

With respect to these three claims I wish to maintain: (1) that the classification of nibbāna as an unconditioned *dhamma* goes back to the most ancient texts and can thus be reasonably assigned to the Buddha himself; (2) that the three-life interpretation of dependent arising, though first made explicit in the commentaries, is clearly and necessarily the Buddha's intention in the suttas; and (3) that while the notion of momentariness is admittedly a later development, the criticism that Joanna levels against it is not valid.

In presenting my case I will be making references to the Pali suttas. I do so in the awareness that Joanna has cast doubt upon the reliability of these sources, suggesting that they may reflect a monastic bias. This is not the place to explore the vexing issue of textual authenticity. Let it suffice to say that despite minor differences in readings and arrangement, the various recensions of the early sutta texts available to us from the non-Theravada schools are in substantial agreement with the Theravada texts in matters of perspective and doctrine, often even the wording is identical. It seems certain that the ascetic and monastic flavor of these documents can be ascribed to the Buddha himself, and not to the special interests of his editors. It must also be remembered that the Buddha adopted the life of a monk to pursue his quest for enlightenment and subsequently established a monastic order for those who would follow him on this quest.

## 2. The Doctrine of Momentariness

I will deal with the three points mentioned above in reverse order. In reply to Joanna's criticism of the idea of momentariness I should first point out that according to the Abhidhamma, the moment during which a dhamma (or factor of experience) exists is not a mathematical point-instant but possesses a certain temporal thickness. Thus the dhamma, though momentary, passes through three fleeting phases: arising, presence, and dissolution. This span of life, however brief, is enough to enable the dhamma to function as a condition for countless other dhammas, and to do so in a wide variety of ways. The analytical method figures prominently in the Abhidhamma as the preliminary tool for dispelling the belief in a solid ego-entity, but it does not exhaust the scope of the Abhidhamma methodology. To the contrary we find that the analytical approach is always counterbalanced and complemented by the synthetic or relational approach, which exhibits the ways that dhammas interact and relate to each other. This project is undertaken in the most painstaking detail in the last book of the Abhidhamma Piṭaka, the Paṭṭhāna, which explores the conditional relations of phenomena in five volumes comprising over 2500 pages. This synthetic approach answers Joanna's objection that the idea of momentariness undermines our conviction that we can exercise an effective presence in the world. By means of its teachings on conditional relations, the Abhidhamma shows that each of our thoughts and actions exercises to some degree a determinative influence on our own future and on the world as a whole.

## 3. The Wheel of Causation

In the Pali suttas the Buddha usually expounds dependent arising (*paṭiccasamuppāda*) as a series of twelve terms each of which is said to arise in dependence on its predecessor. The series, which Joanna calls "the wheel of causation," has become one of the standard formulas of the Dhamma said to comprise the teaching's entire essences. The commentaries assign these twelve factors to three lives: the first two—ignorance and kamma formations—to a preceding life; the last two—birth and aging-and-death—to a subsequent life; and the middle eight factors—consciousness, mind-and-matter, the six sense faculties, contact, feeling, craving, clinging and being—to the intermediate life. Joanna asserts that this three-life interpretation involves a "fundamental shift" away from the Buddha's own conception of the series. I would contend that a study of the many suttas where the Buddha expounds dependent arising would confirm that this three-life interpretation was clearly his intention. In fact, I would hold that apart from this interpretation these suttas, and the series itself, become unintelligible.

Space does not allow for an examination of these suttas here, but such an examination is not even necessary. For the Theravada can rest its case for the three-life interpretation simply by asking what the Buddha's purpose was in teaching this formulation of dependent arising. The Pali suttas make it plain that his purpose was to reveal the causal nexus that keeps us in bondage to saṃsāra, the round of rebirth with all its attendant suffering. The twelve-term formula is then an expository device for neatly laying out the internal dynamics of saṃsāra—for showing what keeps the round in motion and what must be done to make it stop. The extension over three lives serves to show that the ignorance, craving and kammic activity in any given life generate a renewal of existence in the immediately subsequent life, and that those same causal factors, building upon the sensory input of the new life, carry the process of becoming on into still another life.

As the Buddha himself demonstrates (AN 3:61), the formula of dependent arising is actually an expanded version of the second and third noble truths: the forward movement of the series represents the noble truth of the origin of suffering; the reverse movement, by which the ceasing of ignorance effects the cessation of all the following terms, represents the noble truth of the cessation of suffering. To properly appreciate the role of dependent arising in the Buddha's teaching, it always must be viewed in connection with the problem of suffering, and any implications it may have apart from that context are entirely adventitious to the Dhamma.

## 4. The Unconditioned

I will now turn to the first "fundamental shift" that Joanna ascribes to the Theravada, the classification of nibbāna as an unconditioned dhamma. Joanna goes so far as to claim that the very notion of an unconditioned is foreign to the earliest Buddhist teachings. To the contrary I would point out that the Pali suttas affirm in quite unambiguous terms the existence of an unconditioned state, which they hold up as the final goal of the spiritual life. Thus to quote just one pertinent passage: "There is, O monks, an unborn, unmade, unoriginated, unconditioned, without which there would be no escape from the born, made, originated and conditioned" (Ud 8:3). That this unconditioned state is nothing other than nibbāna is underscored by the fact that an entire collection of the Buddha's sayings on the attributes of nibbāna appears in the Pali Canon under the title "Connected Discourses on the Unconditioned" (Asaṅkhata-saṃyutta, SN 43).

In her sketch of the Buddha's philosophical revolution Joanna suggests that the Buddha undercut the prevailing dichotomy of nirvāṇa and saṃsāra by bringing everything real within the scope of change and dependent arising. If the evidence of the Pali suttas is to be trusted, this is not what he did at all. Joanna cites in this connection the Buddha as saying *sabbe aniccā*, "all is impermanent," but what he actually says is "All conditioned things are impermanent" (*sabbe saṅkhārā aniccā*, Dhp 277). He makes this qualification because he affirms the existence of an unconditioned which is not impermanent but imperishable (*accuta*), everlasting (*dhuva*), undecaying (*ajara*), and deathless (*amata*), which exhibits no arising, passing away or change (SN 43, AN 3:47). This does not imply that nibbāna becomes "something abstract, purely mental," a reinforcement of the mind-matter split, as Joanna fears. For the Buddha brings all phenomena both mental and bodily into the sphere of the conditioned, leaving nibbāna as the unconditioned outside the entire complex of mind and body. Nibbāna can be realized within conditioned existence, but in its own nature it is transcendent to everything conditioned and dependently arisen.

It is of prime importance to understand the reason why the notion of the unconditioned claims such a momentous place in the Buddha's teaching. It does so because the Buddha declares that he teaches only two things—suffering and the cessation of suffering (MN 22)—and the unconditioned element, nibbāna, provides the only final and complete cessation of suffering, of dukkha. In its broadest and deepest meaning, the Pali word *dukkha* signifies more than stress, misery and unhappiness. It refers to the inescapably unsatisfactory nature of all existence within the round of rebirths, whether pleasant or painful, because all states of being within the round are impermanent, substanceless, and subject to pain. The Pali suttas testify that far from rejecting the dichotomy of saṃsāra and nibbāna, the Buddha builds his spiritual vision upon this very dichotomy and points out that the goal of the spiritual life is to emerge from the suffering of saṃsāra into the liberation of nibbāna,

Hence the Buddha's solution to the problem of suffering could not consist, as Joanna sees it, in being "released into interbeing, into the dance of the holographic universe, where the part contains the whole." From the standpoint of the Pali suttas, the "holographic universe" is precisely the structure of dukkha: "To one with right view, Kaccāna, who sees the dependent arising of the world, whatever arises is only dukkha arising, whatever ceases is only dukkha ceasing" (SN 12:15). It is true that the Buddha says that the entire world is to found within this six-foot body with its perceptions and consciousness, but he also says that the end of the world is likewise to be found within this same body and that without reaching the end of the world it is impossible to make an end of suffering (SN 2:36).

## 5. THE CONCEPT OF FREEDOM

As an alternative to the understanding of nibbāna as the unconditioned, Joanna explains nibbāna as "the capacity, moment by moment to be free," as freedom "from the attachments and aversions that bind you to small self," This definition is not in principle incompatible with the Theravada account, but from the Theravada point of view it is far from adequate to the conception of liberation set forth in the Pali suttas. There the liberative dimension of nibbāna is said to have two aspects. The first is the nibbāna element with residue remaining, which is the experience of deliverance lived through by the Arahant or Liberated One, attained with the destruction of greed, aversion and delusion. The other aspect is the nibbāna element with no residue remaining, which is the utter release from conditioned existence attained by the Arahant with his final passing away.

There are two significant points to be stressed in this canonical account of liberation. One is that the Arahant's experience of freedom follows from the complete destruction of the three root defilements, and that this destruction has been attained because he has developed his insight into the unsatisfactory nature of conditioned existence to such a level that the defilements have been cut off at the root, unable ever to spring up again. The second point is that the motivation and final goal of the Buddhist spiritual quest is the nibbāna element without residue, and that the nibbāna element with residue enters the picture because it is the closest approach to that possible while the "residue" of bodily existence still remains.

Joanna's conception of nibbānic freedom as moment-by-moment experience falls short of the canonical understanding of nibbāna in both respects. On the one hand she does not seem to recognize that any experience of freedom that does not arise from the total eradication of the mind's defilements will necessarily be incomplete and vulnerable to loss. On the other hand she does not seem to admit the nibbāna element without residue at all. Thus when she says that the Buddha's enlightenment "did not remove him from the world of flux," she overlooks the fact that the main significance of the Buddha's enlightenment in the Pali suttas stems precisely from the liberation it conferred from the flux of repeated birth and death: "The body of the Enlightened One, monks, stands with the leash that bound it to conditioned existence cut. So long as his body stands, gods and men shall see him. But with the breakup of the body and the exhaustion of his life, gods and men shall see him no more" (DN 1).

## 6. The Problem of Escape

Joanna holds, as another criticism of the Theravada, that "when you make nirvana a place to go, a place to be removed from change, then you start to think of this world as a trap and you are always looking for the exit sign. The whole enterprise shifts from transformation of life to escape from life." This characterization of the Theravada position is again open to objection. It is inappropriate, first, to ascribe to Theravada the view that nibbāna is "a place to go" when the tradition never takes that stand; following the Pali suttas the Theravada speaks of nibbāna as a state, element and sphere, but one which necessarily transcends the entire spatiotemporal matrix within which the notion of place acquires meaning.

More serious, however, is the repudiation of the idea of escape, an issue which calls for careful qualification. While Theravada Buddhism does hold up nibbāna as the supreme goal in so far as it constitutes the escape from conditioned existence, this does not mean that it countenances an attitude of flight from the world driven by disappointment, bitterness, or nebulous yearnings for an ideal beyond. Certainly the Theravada would look askance at such pursuits, insisting that a genuine impetus towards liberation must arise in a mature, emotionally balanced individual as a consequence. But what the Theravada would also maintain is that such mature reflection, guided by the Buddha's discourses, would disclose the world to be indeed a "trap" from which we should wisely endeavor to find the exit sign. The noble truth of suffering goes far deeper than Joanna's "terrible trips we play and lay on ourselves." In the Pali suttas the Buddha himself has time and again pointed out that dukkha is built right into the very foundations of the world, in the danger and distress hidden beneath the world's charming exterior; time and again he has praised the blessing in renunciation, in "relinquishing all the foundations of existence." In the famous Fire Sermon he speaks of the world as blazing with the fires of greed, aversion and delusion, with the fires of aging and death. Such being the case, the mission he gives us is not "to fall in love with our world," but to develop dispassion towards all conditioned things and to set our aim at escape from the world (*nissaraṇa*), at nibbāna, which literally means the extinguishment of the flames.

In doing so we need not fear that we will abandon the enterprise of striving for a transformation of life. For in attempting to develop the path that leads to deliverance from the world we will find that a transformation of life naturally sets in, at many levels. What must always be borne in mind is that the path to the unconditioned is a gradual one, which has to be cultivated in stages each of which builds upon its predecessor as its essential foundation—a "transcendental dependent arising." The final realization of the unconditioned does not come about through the anxious flight of the escapist or the smug disillusionment of the cynic, but as the culmination of a total process of training that restructures our entire existential engagement in the world. At a personal level the quest for deliverance requires a full commitment to the Noble Eightfold Path, which involves a wholesale transformation of our views, aims, conduct and mental habits in ways that invariably conduce to the welfare of ourselves and all other beings as well. At wider levels, as the history of Theravada Buddhism during its golden age itself demonstrates, the orientation of society towards the goal of world-transcendence reaches back into the world and promotes the establishment of those social and political structures that are most favorable to wholesome living and provide the optimal external conditions for the inward quest for self-purification.

Far from leaving us callous and resentful towards the world, the pursuit of nibbāna through the eightfold path will inspire generosity, loving kindness, patience, tolerance, humor and devotion to the good of others. Being endowed with the right view that comprehends the Four Noble Truths, we will recognize the dangers and misery inherent in mundane existence and understand the final security from those dangers, the end of suffering, can only be achieved by arriving at the unconditioned, at nibbāna the Deathless. At the same time, because we understand that our fellow beings are likewise caught in the conflagration, we will regard them with boundless kindness and compassion and do our best to alleviate their distress: by providing for their material needs, by offering them protection and freedom from fear, and by helping them to walk the one and only way to final deliverance from suffering.

# Anattā as Strategy and Ontology

## 1. Introduction

This essay will begin as a rejoinder to Ṭhānissaro Bhikkhu's paper, "The Not-self Strategy,"[15] but in the course of commenting on his interpretation of the Buddha's teaching of *anattā*, I will present an alternative view which, I believe, corresponds more closely to the original intent of the texts.

My response to his paper is mixed, part agreement and part disagreement. My disagreements are not minor but stem from a fundamental difference between the views expressed in the paper and my own understanding of the *anattā*-teaching. To state my conclusions in advance: I agree with Ven. Ṭhānissaro that the Buddha did not formulate his teaching of *anattā* as a blank assertion that "There is no self," a claim made by many present-day interpreters of Buddhism. I also agree that the teaching of anattā is intended by the Buddha to fulfill a pragmatic purpose, that it is not a purely philosophical theory but serves as a theme for contemplation. I depart from Ven. Ṭhānissaro over the question whether anattā, even in the early texts, can be satisfactorily understood simply as a "strategy of liberation" without reference to an underlying ontology. I regard the anattā-teaching as both pragmatic and ontological. I do not see these two perspectives as mutually exclusive but, on the contrary, as mutually reinforcing.

What I would maintain, in opposition to Ven. Ṭhānissaro, might be stated briefly as follows. The first three points are closely interwoven and my distinguishing between them is more for the sake of convenience than because the distinctions are cogent.

(1) The reason the teaching of anattā can serve as a strategy of liberation is precisely because it serves to rectify a misconception about the nature of being, hence an ontological error. It accomplishes this task by promoting a correct comprehension of the nature of

15. 1993. Available on the Access to Insight website: www.accessto-insight.org.

being, particularly with reference to our own personal existence.

(2) Without in any way contradicting its practical purposes, the Buddha's teaching of anattā nevertheless involves an implicit ontology, one which precludes a truly existent substantial self. Doctrines that affirm a substantial self are, for the Buddha, instances of wrong view, of a mistaken ontology that ascribes real being to a notion that is a purely conceptual construct without a corresponding basis in actuality. These wrong ontologies are, for the Buddha, obstacles to liberation. Arisen from ignorance and craving, they bend back in a vicious cycle to reinforce our dispositions to craving and clinging. To eliminate craving and clinging, these wrong ontologies have to be corrected. This is what is accomplished by the development of correct wisdom (*sammappaññā*), which exposes phenomena as anattā, as lacking selfhood or any other kind of substantial identity.

(3) The anattā-teaching is a consequence of this ontology, set forth because of its liberative efficacy. Realization of anattā can trigger the experience of awakening, and thereby lead to liberation, precisely because it uncovers the nature of actuality. It is this ontology, the correspondence of the teaching with the actual nature of things, that gives the experience of insight its certainty and finality. Insight into anattā, in other words, is a type of right view (*sammādiṭṭhi*), called "right" because it knows and sees things in accordance with their real nature (*yathābhūtañāṇadassana*).

(4) The distinction between right view and wrong view, between correct understanding and distorted understanding, is not merely provisional, proposed for disciples still in training, but remains valid for the arahant, one who has attained liberation. Even the arahant continues to practice the contemplation of anattā, not to achieve something not yet achieved, but for other benefits this contemplation yields.

Now I will expand on these points.

## 2. THE STRATEGIC FUNCTION OF THE ANATTĀ-TEACHING

Let us first try to see exactly how the teaching of anattā functions as a "strategy of liberation." When anattā is called a liberative strategy, this means more than that it functions therapeutically as a corrective to psychological disease. The teaching of anattā leads to liberation because seeing deeply into the selfless nature of phenomena cuts through the bonds that tie us to saṃsāra, the beginningless round of repeated birth and death. Among the ten "fetters" that hold us in bondage, two involve a mistaken grasp of the nature of our own being. One is personal-identity view (*sakkāyadiṭṭhi*), the view that the five aggregates—either individually or collectively—constitute an *attā*, a substantial self, or stand in an essential relationship to such a self.[16] The other is the conceit "I am" (*asmimāna*), the nebulous sense of an "I" standing in the background of our experience in some undefined relation to the five aggregates. Personal-identity view involves a heavier conceptual overlay and is therefore the coarser of the two. Thus it is eradicated with the attainment of stream-entry, the first of the four stages of ariyan realization. The conceit "I am," being subtler, is also more tenacious. Thus it can be eradicated only with the attainment of the last stage of realization, arahantship.[17] A third defilement that implicitly involves a wrong grasp of the

16. See e.g. Saṃyutta Nikāya 22:82/S III 102: "Bhante, how does identity view come to be?"—"Here, the uninstructed worldling regards form as self, or self as possessing form, or form as in self, or self as in form. He regards feeling as self ... perception as self ... volitional formations as self ... consciousness as self, or self as possessing consciousness, or consciousness as in self, or self as in consciousness. That is how identity view comes to be."

17. For the difference between personal-identity view and the conceit "I am," see especially the Khemaka Sutta (SN 22:89/S III 126–132). Here the monk Khemaka explains to a group of monks: "Friends, even though a noble disciple has abandoned the five lower fetters [including personal-identity view], still, in relation to the five aggregates, there lingers in him a residual conceit 'I am,' a desire 'I am,' an underlying tendency 'I am' that has not yet been uprooted. Sometime later he dwells contemplating rise and fall in the five aggregates. As he does so, the residual conceit 'I am,' the desire 'I am,' the underlying tendency 'I am' is uprooted."

nature of being is craving, on account of which we hold to the five aggregates as "mine."

As long as the mind is governed by these underlying tendencies, we constantly construe our experience in terms of the notions of "I," "mine," and "my self." In the grip of wrong view and conceit, we take the five aggregates to be "I" and "my self." In the grip of craving we cling to the aggregates as "mine," seeking to widen the boundaries of our personal domain by appropriating as much as we can of the external world. The contemplation of anattā fulfills a strategic role by undermining the mental grip of personal-identity view, conceit, and craving. Whereas the "uninstructed worldling" is prone to regard each element of experience—form, feeling, perception, volitions, and consciousness—thus: "This is mine, I am this, this is myself," the "instructed noble disciple" reverses this whole process of conceiving by viewing all experience thus: "This is not mine, I am not this, this is not my self." This contemplation, methodically developed, sets in motion a gradual dis-identification with the five aggregates which, coming to a head, eradicates first, at the stage of stream-entry, the fetter of personal-identity view, and subsequently, at the stage of arahantship, craving and the conceit "I am."

This discussion helps us to understand why the Buddha did not formulate anattā as a simple denial of the self, with the assertion, "There is no self." To correct our deeply ingrained tendencies to identify things as "self" and to appropriate them as "mine," a simple declaration, "There is no self," would have been powerless and could even have brought confusion to the listener. The problem the Buddha addresses with the teaching of anattā is our habitual identification of things as "I" and "mine," as a self and the belongings of a self. Such acts of identification seem justified in so far as things do appear to us as "I" and "mine." They present themselves to perception as a self and the belongings of a self. The effective antidote is not to deny outright the mistaken term of ascription by maintaining, "There is no self," but to demonstrate that our identification of things as a self is an error, a mis-identification, a mistake in the literal sense of "taking up wrongly."

The anattā-teaching is offered as the means to correct this wrong identification. The Buddha usually approaches the task of correcting this error in an indirect manner. He first gets us to confirm that the things identified as a self are impermanent and unreliable. Then he makes us see that because they are impermanent and unreliable it is untenable for us to consider them as a self or the belongings of a self. The presupposition underlying this argument is that whatever is taken to be a self must be lasting and reliable, an inviolable source of happiness. Since the five aggregates (or the twelve sense bases or eighteen elements, alternative ways of analyzing experience) are impermanent and vulnerable to suffering, the conclusion follows that they are not a self. Thus, the texts repeatedly tell us, whatever is taken as a self must be seen with proper wisdom as it really is thus: "This is not mine, I am not this, this is not my self."

## 3. The Anattā-Teaching Rests on an Ontology

So far I have simply been explaining the strategic function of the teaching of anattā. I have not yet shown exactly where I differ from Ven. Ṭhānissaro. Now I will explain where I differ from him. Ven. Ṭhānissaro holds that the teaching of anattā is entirely strategic, without any ontological ramifications. I see the teaching of anattā as resting on an ontology.

Let me begin by calling attention to the fact that the three defilements responsible for conceptions of selfhood—personal-identity view, craving, and the conceit "I am"—all arise from ignorance (*avijjā*), which is defined in the suttas as not knowing and not seeing things as they really are. This definition is elaborated by the texts in various ways. Thus it is said to be not knowing suffering, its origin, cessation, and the path. It is not knowing form, feeling, perception, volitional activities, and consciousness, their arising and their ceasing. It is not knowing the eye, ear, nose, tongue, body and mind, their arising and ceasing; not knowing their objects, their respective types of consciousness, etc., their arising and their ceasing (see SN 22:126–35/III 171–76). Thus, while it is true that the Buddha taught anattā because it corrects our self-centered clinging and thus serves a "strategic" purpose, the teaching of anattā does not operate in an ontological vacuum but rests on an appeal to the actual nature of things, which serves as its foundation.

It is from this foundation that anattā draws both its effectiveness and its validity. This ontological foundation is, however, at the same time an ontological vacuity. The teaching is not intended to establish the existence of some reality beyond the range of experience, but to demonstrate the absence, or non-existence, of anything within experience—either among the five aggregates or apart from them—that meets the criterion of true selfhood. That is, what it denies is that the five aggregates contain a permanent, stable, blissful core of personal identity.

Because the Buddha intends his teaching to be "emancipating" (*niyyānika*), to lead to liberating insight and detachment, he does not state the underlying ontology in the abstract. However, contrary to Ven. Ṭhānissaro, I would not stop at describing the teaching of anattā as essentially a "technique of perception." I would emphasize instead that contemplation of anattā generates a perception *that accords with the actual nature of things*. I would maintain that it is precisely the correspondence between this perception and the actual nature of things that ensures that the detachment effected by the perception is complete and irreversible. The texts describe the insight into anattā by the expression "knowing and seeing things as they really are" (*yathābhūtañāṇadassana*). Here, the term *yathābhūta*, "as they really are," underscores the accuracy of the perception, its correspondence to actuality. The perception is not merely an expedient technique with therapeutic benefits, but an insight that cuts through conceptual and perceptual distortions to uncover phenomena in their own nature. Thus, when a monk came to the Buddha and asked, "How should one know and see so that there is no more I-making, mine-making, and underlying tendencies to conceit in regard to this body with its consciousness and in regard to all external objects?", the Buddha replied:

> "Whatever form there is past, present, and future, internal or external, (etc.), *one sees all form as it really is with correct wisdom thus*: 'This is not mine, this I am not, this is not my self.' Whatever feeling ... perception ... volitional activities ... consciousness there are past, present, and future (etc.), *one sees all consciousness as it really is with correct wisdom thus*: 'This is not mine, this I am not, this is not my self.'? Knowing and seeing thus, there is no more I-making, mine-making, and underlying tendencies to conceit in regard to this body with its consciousness and in regard to all external objects."[18]

18. MN 109/M III 18–19: "*Yaṃ kiñci, bhikkhu, rūpaṃ—atītānāgatapaccuppannaṃ ajjhattaṃ vā bahiddhā vā oḷārikaṃ vā sukhumaṃ vā hīnaṃ vā paṇītaṃ*

In my understanding, the words "seeing as it really is with correct wisdom" indicate that this is not merely a strategic perception but one that derives its efficacy from its correspondence to actuality.

There is one further comment I want to make on the first section of Ven. Ṭhānissaro's paper. With reference to the Vacchagotta dialogue (and later in connection with the passage from MN 2 quoted in section 3 of his essay), he defends his interpretation by pointing out that the Buddha actually rejected the thesis, "There is no self." In doing so, however, he does not mention that there is a significant difference between the view "there is no self" advocated in these suttas and the interpretation of anattā as meaning "there in no self" advanced by recent exponents of early Buddhism. The proposition "there is no self" repudiated by the Buddha in these suttas is *not* offered as a possible formulation of the anattā-teaching, one that the Buddha is rejecting. As the discussion with Vacchagotta makes clear, the proposition "there is no self" was the position maintained by the annihilationists (*ucchedavādin*), the materialist philosophers who held that death marks the complete end of personal existence. The annihilationists assume that the existence of a self—a permanent *ātman*—is a necessary condition for an afterlife and the operation of kamma; thus by denying the existence of such a self, they intend to reject any type of afterlife along with its corollary, the moral efficacy of kammic action.

When the Buddha refuses to accept the annihilationist thesis that "there is no self," he refuses because he cannot consent to the consequences the annihilationists wish to draw from such a denial, namely, that there is no conscious survival beyond the present life. In contrast, when modern interpreters of Buddhism take *anattā* to mean "there is no self," they are not saying that the anattā-teaching entails the annihilation of the person at death. Rather, they are simply trying to state in the abstract the premise that underlies the

---

*vā yaṃ dūre santike vā—sabbaṃ rūpaṃ 'netaṃ mama, nesohamasmi, na meso attā'ti—evametaṃ yathābhūtaṃ sammappaññāya passati. Yā kāci vedanā... yā kāci saññā... ye keci saṅkhārā... yaṃ kiñci viññāṇaṃ—atītānāgatapaccuppannaṃ ajjhattaṃ vā bahiddhā vā oḷārikaṃ vā sukhumaṃ vā hīnaṃ vā paṇītaṃ vā yaṃ dūre santike vā—sabbaṃ viññāṇaṃ 'netaṃ mama, nesohamasmi, na meso attā'ti—evametaṃ yathābhūtaṃ sammappaññāya passati. Evaṃ kho, bhikkhu, jānato evaṃ passato imasmiñca saviññāṇake kāye bahiddhā ca sabbanimittesu ahaṃkāramamaṃ-kāramānānusayā na hontī''ti.*

Buddha's more concrete instructions on the contemplation of non-self. While this assertion may go beyond the way the anattā-teaching is expressed in the suttas, it is not proper to support one's argument by identifying the position of the modern interpreters with the annihilationist doctrine found in the Nikāyas and then point to the Buddha's rejection of the annihilationist view as ipso facto implying rejection of the other. The purport of the two is altogether different, and to identify them while aware of the difference seems to be a disingenuous move.

## 4. THE ONTOLOGY OF THE CONDITIONED

Although, as I indicated just above, the Dhamma is not a mere philosophy divorced from practice, we can nevertheless see in the Buddha's discourses an implicit ontology. At the risk of misunderstanding, I will offer a brief sketch of this ontology in order to show why it excludes any theoretical view of self. The ontology that emerges from a study of the Nikāyas draws a fundamental distinction between two types of realities, the conditioned and the unconditioned. Conditioned reality comprises everything arisen from conditions; it includes all existents classified into such schemes as the five aggregates, the twelve sense bases, the eighteen elements, etc. We need not go along with the commentaries in taking these entities to exist by reason of some kind of "intrinsic nature" (*sabhāva*), a notion that does shade off into the arena of metaphysical hypothesis. We can simply take the ontology to acknowledge the bare existence of the elements of experience. The Buddha says that all conditioned reality is distinguished by three "characteristics of the conditioned" (*saṅkhatalakkhaṇa*): its arising is discerned, its falling away is discerned, and its alteration while it persists is discerned (AN 3:47/A I 152). In contrast, the unconditioned is characterized by the three "characteristics of the unconditioned" (*asaṅkhatalakkhaṇa*): no arising is discerned, no falling away is discerned, and no alteration while persisting is discerned. While many conditioned realities are enumerated in the suttas, only one unconditioned is recognized, nibbāna.

In his discourses the Buddha classifies conditioned phenomena in diverse ways, into such schemes as the five aggregates, the twelve sense bases, the eighteen elements, and so forth. These all represent the same broad range of "dhammas," which are merely distributed into different categories. The most common scheme is that of the five aggregates, for the texts say that whenever we identify anything as a self, the object so identified is one or another of the five aggregates of clinging: "Whatever recluses or brahmins recognize a self in various ways, all recognize the five aggregates of clinging or a certain one among them" (SN 22:47/S III 46). Although one may posit in thought a self transcendent to the five aggregates—as a reality altogether beyond the mind-body complex and its activities—when one seeks to provide some *content to the idea of self*, to substantiate the term with a content, one can only do so with reference to one or another of the five aggregates (or to the aggregates as a composite whole). The self is either form, or possessed of form, or in form, or the container of form; and so too for feeling, perception, the volitional activities, and consciousness. Since the basis for views of self is the five aggregates, to break this identification the Buddha points to the five aggregates as the sphere for the contemplation of anattā.[19]

The reason none of these conditioned entities is self follows from the ontology of the conditioned. Whatever is conditioned bears the "characteristics of the conditioned": arising, falling away, and alteration. But if that conditioned entity, being subject to arising and falling away, were to be regarded as self, it would follow that one's self arises and falls away, and in the Buddha's understanding, this undercuts its identification as self, which must be permanent and unchanging. The argument is presented most clearly in the Discourse on the Six Sets of Six, where the Buddha begins with the six sense faculties as the subject of inquiry:

> "If anyone should say that the eye is self, that would not be tenable. For an arising and a falling away of the eye are discerned. But since its arising and falling away are discerned, it would follow that "my self arises and falls away." Therefore it would not be tenable for one to say that the eye is self. Thus the eye is not self."[20]

---

19. Along with the five aggregates, we should add the twelve sense bases and the eighteen elements, which are simply alternative schemes for classifying conditioned phenomena.

20. MN 148/M III 282–83: "'*Cakkhu attā'ti yo vadeyya taṃ na upapajjati. Cakkhussa uppādopi vayopi paññāyati. Yassa kho pana uppādopi vayopi*

An "ontological dissonance" thus emerges between the *basis for the ascription of selfhood*, namely, the conditioned entities comprised in the five aggregates, the twelve sense bases, and the eighteen elements, and *the term of ascription*, namely, existence as a self, which implies unchanging persistence through time. Because the conditioned realities identified as self arise and fall away, they do not measure up to the notion of selfhood, which is a mode of being that involves stability, the absence of arising and passing away. From this ontological dissonance the insight is born that the basis of ascription is not what it is conceived to be; in other words, that the phenomena conceived to be self are actually anattā, not-self. This point is expressed pungently in a pair of verses from the Dvayatānupassanā Sutta of the Suttanipāta:

> Behold the world together with its deities
> conceiving a self in what is non-self.
> Settled upon name-and-form,
> they conceive: "This is true."
> In whatever way they conceive it,
> it turns out otherwise than the way [it is conceived].
> That indeed is its falsity,
> for the transient is of a deceptive nature.[21]

---

*paññāyati, 'attā me uppajjati ca veti cā'ti iccassa evamāgataṃ hoti. Tasmā taṃ na upapajjati—'cakkhu attā'ti yo vadeyya. Iti cakkhu anattā.*" The same is said about forms, eye-consciousness, eye-contact, feeling arisen from eye-contact, and craving for forms, and about all the other sense faculties and their associated phenomena.

21. Sn 756–57 (Be 761–62): *Anattani attamāniṃ passa lokaṃ sadevakaṃ; niviṭṭhaṃ nāmarūpasmiṃ, idaṃ saccanti maññati. Yena yena hi maññanti, tato taṃ hoti aññathā; taṃ hi tassa musā hoti, mosadhammaṃ hi ittaraṃ.*

## 5. WHY IS THE ANATTĀ-TEACHING EFFECTIVE?

That the strategic effectiveness of the anattā-teaching derives from its ontological "groundedness" can be brought to light more clearly if we consider that the contemplation of anattā, when fully developed, *eradicates* even the latent tendencies towards personal-identity view, craving, and conceit. The contemplation would not be capable of such an achievement if its efficacy were fully exhausted by its strategic role in countering self-identification. The penetration of the characteristic of anattā does not merely debilitate the defilements or hold them in check. It cuts them off at their very roots, so that they an never arise again in the future.

In my view, this capacity of the contemplation of anattā derives from its connection with the underlying ontology. The contemplation draws its efficacy from its correspondence with the actual nature of things. As I understand it, the contemplation of anattā, as it gradually develops, draws closer and closer to alignment with the actual nature of things, and as it does so, it counters and inhibits the mind's proclivities towards conceiving in terms of self. But even in this phase the perception of anattā, as clear as it may be, is not yet capable of eradicating those tendencies. It is only when this contemplation reaches its apex—when it becomes *perfectly aligned* with the actual nature of things—that the inner realization takes place that sets the meditator irreversibly on the definite path to liberation. This event, which the texts call the breakthrough to the Dhamma (*dhammābhisamaya*) or the arising of the eye of Dhamma (*dhammacakkhu*), marks the attainment of stream-entry, the first stage of noble realization, which sets the disciple on course to attain final liberation in a maximum of seven more lives, with no possibility of a relapse. Although the Pali Nikāyas do not abound in explicit ontological terminology, I feel that the expressions they use to describe this experience suggest that the contemplation of anattā, which culminates in the arising of the "eye of Dhamma," draws its efficacy from its "ontological alignment" with the true nature of the objects of contemplation. And that "true nature" is precisely the absence in them of any substantial selfhood, any enduring core of personal identity.

To highlight the difference between a purely strategic mode of perception and a mode of perception that is both strategic and ontologically grounded, we might compare the types of perceptions used in the meditation on loving-kindness (*mettābhāvanā*) and the meditation on foulness (*asubhabhāvanā*) with the type of perception involved in the contemplation of anattā. In the former two kinds of meditation, a meditator counteracts defilements by developing particular perceptions that do not have any ontological implications at all. Thus to develop loving-kindness, one endeavors to perceive other beings as dear and lovable. By doing so, one engenders a wish for their welfare and happiness—the salient quality of loving-kindness—and this helps to remove the mental stain of ill will. To develop dispassion for sensual pleasures, one examines the thirty-two parts of the body—the head-hairs, body-hairs, nails, teeth, skin, bones, and so forth—viewing each part as repulsive. When the repulsiveness of the body is seen, lust for sensual pleasure is abandoned. Although this examination reveals genuine features of the body ordinarily hidden from view, these features are still not real in an ontological sense. The perception of the body as foul does not see the body in basic ontological terms, as consisting of "bare phenomena" (*suddhadhamma*) or mere elements (*dhātumatta*) that are dependently arisen, subject to arising and falling away in accordance with conditions.

The perception of beings as lovable, essential to the meditation on loving-kindness, and the perception of the body as repulsive, the core of the meditation on foulness, are both '"strategies of perception" that promote wholesome qualities and conduce to mental purification. The one helps to remove ill will, the other to remove sensual lust. However, while these perceptions remove the opposed defilements, they do so only temporarily; they cannot *eradicate* the defilements and thus do not directly lead to unshakable liberation of the mind. I would maintain that the reason their impact is limited is because they do not reach down to the fundamental ontological level. They do not involve "knowing and seeing with proper wisdom things as they really are."

In contrast, the perception of anattā not only temporarily removes false conceptions of selfhood—the notions of "I" and "self"—but when fully developed it permanently eradicates the "fetters" of personal-identity view and conceit that underlie such notions. Even more, the perception of anattā also eradicates the *emotional afflictions* of sensual passion and ill will, which can only be checked by the meditations on foulness and loving-kindness.

While the latter temporarily suppress them, it takes insight into anattā to permanently eliminate them.

This is the case because all these defilements ultimately spring from ignorance, from a failure to comprehend the real nature of things, and they therefore must finally be removed by wisdom, by correct insight into the real nature of things. Such insight could make no claim to being a truthful cognition—to being in attunement with things as they actually are—if it did not have an ontological basis. The contemplation of anattā can bring forth the "eye of Dhamma" and give rise to the liberative path precisely because it uncovers, at increasingly deeper and subtler levels, the actual nature of phenomena. Admittedly, this ontology is quite different from other types of ontology, since it is not designed to establish the being or reality of things but to expose the unreality of a false notion, to correct a mistaken way of construing the nature of existent phenomena. But in so far as the teaching on anattā is intended to make known the real nature of things, the way things actually exist, it necessarily involves an ontological dimension.

## 6. The Right View of the Arahant

I will conclude by dealing with one further point in Ven. Ṭhānissaro's paper, his contention that "for the Tathāgata ... views are neither true nor false, but simply phenomena to be experienced.... Views of true, false, self, no self, etc., thus lose all their holding power, and the mind is left free to its Suchness" (p.?7). To support this conclusion he appeals to some evocative verses in the Kālakārāma Sutta (AN 4:24/A II 24–25) and the Suttanipāta, but it seems questionable that the texts he appeals to can bear the weight of the interpretation that he ascribes to them. As a general rule, to uncover the doctrinal positions of the early texts, we are on more secure ground when we rely on the prose suttas, which aim at lucid exposition rather than poetic suggestion. The prose texts make it plain that the Buddha and the arahants affirm the clear distinction between right view and wrong view and repeatedly insist that we should equip ourselves with the former and reject the latter.

Whether in verse or in prose, the Buddha does teach that we should not cling tenaciously to any view, even right view. Thus, with regard to the view of dependent origination, he says: "If you adhere to this view, treasure it and treat it as a possession, then you would not understand the Dhamma that has been taught as similar to a raft, being for the purpose of crossing over, not for the purpose of grasping" (MN 38/M I 260–61). There is a major difference, however, between, on the one hand, asserting that views are neither true nor false but simply phenomena to be experienced, and on the other, asserting that views are true and false and that false views are to be rejected and true views adopted without clinging to them. The suttas that are explicit in meaning indicate that the latter attitude, not the former one, is the one the Buddha advocates.

Moreover, the Nikāyas nowhere say that right view is to be discarded by the arahants. Arahants have, in a sense, transcended right view, in that they have brought to a conclusion the primary function of right view as a path factor. But this does not mean that they discard right view. The texts mention ten qualities possessed by the arahant: the eight factors of the noble eightfold path, augmented by right knowledge and right liberation. The first of these ten qualities is "the right view of one beyond training" (*asekhā sammādiṭṭhi*, see MN 65/MI 446; MN 78/M II 29), "one beyond training" being an arahant. Since the texts do not define the content of "right view of one beyond training," it seems safe to assume that its content is the same as the right view of the disciple on the path. In both cases, it is the understanding of the four noble truths, dependent origination, and the three characteristics of phenomena. The only difference between them would be in function. While the right view of the disciple in training is a factor *of the path*, to be used to reach the goal of the path, for the arahant—who has reached the end of the path—it no longer aims at the eradication of defilements but is simply an inalienable endowment.

Yet arahants continue to make use of their right view, and several texts even indicate they may continue to practice the contemplation of anattā. This seems to be another point against the thesis that anattā serves solely a strategic function. If its function were solely to rectify such wrong ideas as "I" and "mine," the arahant, who has overcome all such notions, would no longer have any occasion to resort to the contemplation of anattā. Yet the Venerable Sāriputta states the contrary:

Even an arahant, friend, should wisely attend to these five aggregates of clinging as impermanent, as suffering, as a sickness, a boil, a dart, as misery, as disease, as alien, as disintegrating, as empty, *as not self*. For the arahant there is nothing further to be done nor any need to repeat what he has done, but these things, developed and cultivated, lead to a pleasant abiding here and now and to mindfulness and clear comprehension.[22]

22. SN 22:122/S III 168–69: *Arahatāpi kho, āvuso koṭṭhita, ime pañcupādānakkhandhe aniccato dukkhato rogato gaṇḍato sallato aghato ābādhato parato palokato suññato anattato yoniso manasi kātabbā. Natthi, khvāvuso, arahato uttari karaṇīyaṃ katassa vā paticayo; api ca ime dhammā bhāvitā bahulīkatā diṭṭha-dhamma--sukhavihārā ceva saṃvattanti satisampajaññā ca.* See too SN 22:123/S III 169.

# A Critical Examination of Ñāṇavīra Thera's "*A Note on Paṭiccasamuppāda*"

## 1. Introduction

Ñāṇavīra Thera's *Notes on Dhamma* was first published in 1963, during the author's lifetime, in a small cyclostyled edition distributed to a select list of recipients. During the following two years the author made a number of corrections and substantial additions to his original text, leaving behind at his death an enlarged typescript entitled *Notes on Dhamma (1960–1965)*. For twenty-two years this version circulated from hand to hand among a small circle of readers in the form of typed copies, photocopies, and handwritten manuscripts. Only in 1987 did *Notes on Dhamma* appear in print, when it was issued along with a collection of the author's letters under the title *Clearing the Path: Writings of Ñāṇavīra Thera (1960–1965)*.[23]

Even this edition, a print run of 1,000 copies, turned out to be ephemeral. Barely nine months after the book was released, the editor-publisher (who had invested at least five years preparing the material for publication) died under tragic circumstances. Path Press effectively closed down, and the question whether the book will ever be reprinted still hangs in the air. But in spite of its limited availability, *Clearing the Path* has had an impact on its readers that has been nothing short of electric. Promoted solely by word of mouth, the book has spawned an international network

23. *Notes on Dhamma* is available on www.nanavira.org and *Clearing the Path* on www.buddhanet.net.

of admirers—a Theravāda Buddhist underground—united in their conviction that *Notes on Dhamma* is the sole key to unlock the inner meaning of the Buddha's Teaching. Some of its admirers have called it the most important book written in this century, others have hailed it as the most outstanding work on the Dhamma to appear since the Nikāyas were first written down on palm leaves at the Aluvihāra. For the book's enthusiasts no effort is too much in struggling through its dense pages of tightly compressed arguments and copious Pāli quotations in order to fulfill its author's invitation "to come and share his point of view."

Ven. Ñāṇavīra's purpose in writing the *Notes* was, in his own words, "to indicate the proper interpretation of the Suttas," the key to which he believed he had discovered through an experience that he identified as the arising of the Eye of Dhamma (*dhammacakkhu*), that is, the attainment of stream-entry. His proposition sounds innocuous enough as it stands, until one discovers that the author sees this task as entailing nothing less than a radical revaluation of the entire Theravāda exegetical tradition. Few of the standard interpretative principles upheld by Theravāda orthodoxy are spared the slashing of his pen. The most time-honored explanatory tools for interpreting the Suttas, along with the venerated books from which they stem, he dismisses as "a mass of dead matter choking the Suttas." The Abhidhamma-piṭaka, the *Milindapañha*, the *Visuddhimagga*, the Pāli Commentaries—all come in for criticism, and the author says that ignorance of them "may be counted a positive advantage as leaving less to be unlearned."

Strangely, although *Notes on Dhamma* makes such a sharp frontal attack on Theravāda orthodoxy, to date no proponent of the mainstream Theravāda tradition has risen to the occasion and attempted to counter its arguments. The few traditionalists who have read the book have either disregarded it entirely or merely branded it as a thicket of errors. But to my knowledge, none has tried to point out exactly what these errors are and to meet its criticisms with reasoned argumentation based directly on the texts.

The present essay is an attempt to fill that gap. I will be concerned here with only one note in Ven. Ñāṇavīra's collection, his "*A Note on Paṭiccasamuppāda.*" This note, however, is the main pillar of Ven. Ñāṇavīra's distinctive approach to the Suttas; it is the first and longest note in the book and the most consistently radical.

The Note sounds a bold challenge to the prevailing "three-life interpretation" of the twelve-factored formula of dependent arising. The traditional interpretation of this formula, expounded in full detail in the Visuddhimagga (Chapter XVII), has guided followers of mainstream Theravāda Buddhism for centuries in their understanding of this most profound and difficult principle of the Dhamma. Hence a criticism of it that claims to be validated by the Suttas themselves strikes from within at the very core of the orthodox Theravāda commentarial tradition.

At the beginning of his Note, Ven. Ñāṇavīra states that he assumes his reader is acquainted with this traditional interpretation and is dissatisfied with it (§2). Such dissatisfaction, he asserts, is not unjustified, and he proposes to provide in its place what he modestly claims "may perhaps be found to be a more satisfactory approach." I too will assume that the reader is already acquainted with the three-life interpretation, and hence I will not recapitulate that interpretation here. While the reader who has personal access to Ven. Ñāṇavīra's Note and can refer to it in the course of this discussion may be able to follow my arguments here more easily, for the benefit of readers who are not so situated I will recount below those contentions of his with which I take issue.

My purpose in writing this examination is to vindicate the traditional three-life interpretation against Ven. Ñāṇavīra's critique of it. I propose to show that the approach which he considers to be "more satisfactory" not only cannot be justified by reference to the discourses of the Buddha, but is in fact flatly contradicted by those discourses. I also intend to establish that, contrary to Ven. Ñāṇavīra's allegations, the three-life interpretation, though not explicitly stated in such terms, is fully in accord with the Buddha's teachings. In my view, this interpretation, far from deviating from the Suttas, simply makes explicit the Buddha's intention in expounding dependent arising.

In making this assertion, I am not saying that the detailed exposition of *paṭicca-samuppāda* (PS) as found in the Pāli Commentaries can in all particulars be traced back to the Suttas. The aim of the Commentaries, in their treatment of PS, is to correlate the Suttanta teaching of PS with the systematic analysis of phenomena and their conditional relations as found in the Abhidhamma. This results in an explanation of PS that is far more complex and technical than anything that can be drawn out from the Sutta texts themselves. I do not think that acceptance of the basic dynamics of the "three-life" approach entails acceptance of all the details of the commentarial explanation, and I also believe that the Commentaries take unnecessary risks when they try to read back into the Suttas ideas deriving from tools of interpretation that appeared perhaps centuries after the Suttas were compiled. All that I wish to maintain is that the essential vision underlying the commentarial interpretation is correct: namely, that the twelvefold formula of PS extends over three lives and as such describes the generative structure of *saṃsāra*, the round of repeated births.

Like Ven. Ñāṇavīra, I take as the sole ultimate authority for interpretation of the Dhamma the Buddha's discourses as found in the four main Nikāyas and in the older strata of the Khuddaka Nikāya. I share with Ven. Ñāṇavīra the view that these books can be considered the most trustworthy record of the Buddha's teachings, and hence should be turned to as the final court of appeal for resolving questions about the correct interpretation of the Dhamma. Unlike Ven. Ñāṇavīra, however, I do not hold that all later works, such as the Abhidhamma-piṭaka and the Commentaries, should be rejected point blank as miasmas of error and decay. We must certainly accept the findings of scientific scholarship regarding the dating of the canonical and post-canonical texts, and should recognize that Theravāda doctrine has evolved in several strata through the Abhidhamma, the Commentaries, and the later exegetical works. In my view, however, this does not mean that every text that was composed after the age of the Nikāyas must be regarded with distrust or disdain.

## 2. FUNDAMENTAL ATTITUDES

Before I turn to examine specific points in Ven. Ñāṇavīra's Note I wish to focus on one discomfiting consequence entailed by his insistence that his view of *paṭicca-samuppāda* is exclusively and absolutely correct. The three-life interpretation of *paṭicca-samuppāda* has been maintained by the Theravāda tradition virtually from the time that tradition emerged as a distinct school. It goes back long before the time of Buddhaghosa's commentaries and can be found already in near-definitive form in the Vibhaṅga of the Abhidhamma-piṭaka and the Paṭisambhidāmagga of the Sutta-piṭaka, works dating from around the 3rd century BC. Further, this interpretation, in its essential outlines, is by no means peculiar to the Theravāda school. It was also shared, with minor differences in details, by the early rivals of the Theravāda, the Sarvāstivāda and Mahāsāṃghika, which suggests that at least in outline this way of explaining *paṭicca-samuppāda* already preceded the first schisms. The same three-life division can be found in the works of the great Mādhyamika philosopher Nāgārjuna (e.g. in his *Mūla-mādhyamika-kārikā*, chapter 26), and is also held in the present day by the Mahāyāna schools that have inherited the exegetical methodology of ancient Indian Buddhism.

In contrast, Ven. Ñāṇavīra's view of *paṭicca-samuppāda*, as pertaining solely to a single life, appears to be without a precedent in the tenet systems of early Buddhism. Thus, when Ven. Ñāṇavīra holds that he has correctly grasped the Buddha's intention in expounding PS, this implicitly commits him to the thesis that the entire mainstream Buddhist philosophical tradition has utterly misinterpreted this most fundamental Buddhist doctrine, and had already done so within two centuries after the Master's demise. While it is not altogether impossible that this had occurred, it would seem a lapse of an astonishing magnitude on the part of the early Buddhist community.

Of course, the above argument is not in itself compelling, for one might still be prepared to stand behind Ven. Ñāṇavīra's claim no matter how audacious it may be. So let us now turn to the Note itself and examine his views on *paṭicca-samuppāda*. For the present we will pass over his opening salvos against the three-life interpretation. Instead, let us move directly into the sections of the Note in which he reveals his own "more satisfactory approach." We will return to the criticisms later and see if they truly require us to abandon the traditional understanding of the doctrine.

Ven. Ñāṇavīra maintains that *paṭicca-samuppāda*, in its twelve-factored formulation, applies solely and entirely to our existential situation in this present life, without any reference to temporal divisions. It is, in his view, an ever-present existential structure of the unenlightened mind describing the mode of being of the "uninstructed common person" (*assutavā puthujjana*). Ven. Ñāṇavīra insists that this interpretation of PS alone offers us a way to resolve the immediate problem of existence in the present itself: "It is a matter of one's fundamental attitude to one's own existence—is there, or is there not, a present problem, or rather, anxiety that can only be resolved in the present?" (§7).

I fully agree with Ven. Ñāṇavīra that our interpretation of *paṭicca-samuppāda* must flow from our "fundamental attitude to (our) own existence." It is also clear from the Suttas that the Buddha's motive in teaching PS is to lead us to a present resolution of the existential problem of suffering. Repeatedly in the Suttas we see the Buddha teaching PS in order to lay bare the structure of conditions that underlies the origination and cessation of dukkha. However, in order to understand how *paṭicca-samuppāda* fulfils this function, we should focus on the question: What is the meaning of the dukkha that the Buddha's Teaching is designed to liberate us from? Ven. Ñāṇavīra contends that this dukkha is the anxiety and stress that pervades our present existence, and hence he interprets all the terms of the standard PS formula in a way that lends support to this contention. But if we read the Suttas on their own terms, in their totality, we would find that Ven. Ñāṇavīra's understanding of dukkha falls far short of the vision of the first noble truth that the Buddha wishes to impart to us. Of course, dukkha does include "existential anxiety," and there are several suttas which define the conditions for the arising and removal of such dukkha. An unbiased and complete survey of the Nikāyas, however, would reveal that the problem of dukkha to which the Buddha's Teaching is addressed is not primarily existential anxiety, nor even the distorted sense of self of which such anxiety may be symptomatic. The primary problem of dukkha with which the Buddha is concerned, in its most comprehensive and fundamental dimensions, is the problem of our bondage to *saṃsāra*—the round of repeated birth, aging, and death. And, as I will show presently, these terms are intended quite literally as signifying biological birth, aging, and death, not our anxiety over being born, growing old, and dying.

A glance at the Suttas would suffice to reveal to us the "fundamental attitudes" that motivated the Buddha and the early disciples in their own quest for deliverance. We find, for example, that each Bodhisatta, from Vipassī to Gotama, seeks the path to enlightenment with the thought, "Alas, this world has fallen into trouble, in that it is born and ages and dies and passes away and is reborn, and it does not know of the escape from this suffering of aging and death." When young seekers go forth into homelessness out of faith in the Buddha, they do so because they have realized: "I am immersed in birth, aging and death, sorrow, lamentation, pain, displeasure, and despair; I am immersed in suffering, afflicted with suffering. Perhaps one can discern here an end-making to this entire mass of suffering." Again and again the Buddha stresses the misery of repeated existence within *saṃsāra*, again and again he underscores the urgency of escaping from it (see e.g. SN Ch. 15/S II 178–93). And his constant injunction to the monks throughout his ministry was to dwell diligently so that "having abandoned the cycle of births, you will make an end of suffering." These words should leave no doubt that by putting an end to suffering the Buddha means—not release from existential anxiety—but release from the round of rebirths. In so far as the Dhamma addresses the problem of our present suffering, it does so by situating that suffering in its larger context, our condition of saṃsāric bondage. The present cannot be considered only in its vertical depths. It must also be viewed as the intersection of the past and future, shaped by our past experience and harboring our future destiny in its womb.

If the Dhamma is to enable us to extricate ourselves from the dukkha of repeated birth and death, it must make known the chain of causes that holds us in bondage to this round of repeated birth and death, and it must also indicate what must be done to bring this cycle to a halt. Throughout the Suttas we can find only one basic statement of the causal structure of *saṃsāra*, one overarching formulation with many minor variations, and that is the twelvefold formula of dependent arising. If one's aim in following the Dhamma is to gain release from existential anxiety, then the three-life interpretation of PS may seem unsatisfactory and one may turn to Ven. Ñāṇavīra's version as more adequate. But the task which the Buddha sets before his disciples is of a different nature: namely, to gain liberation from the recurrent cycle of birth, old age, and death, that is, from bondage to *saṃsāra*. Once one accepts this task as one's own, one will then see that PS must be looked upon as a disclosure of the conditional structure of *saṃsāra*, showing us how our ignorance, craving, and volitional activity keep us chained to the round of existence and drive us from one life to the next.

## 3. BIRTH, AGING AND DEATH

I now intend to take up for scrutiny what might be regarded as the two main planks of Ven. Ñāṇavīra's interpretation. The two planks to which I am referring are his attempts to explain the relationships between those conditions which, in the traditional interpretation, are held to extend over different lifetimes. These are: (i) the nexus of *bhava*, *jāti*, and *jarāmaraṇa*—becoming ('being', in Ven. Ñāṇavīra's translation), birth, and aging-and-death; and (ii) the nexus of *avijjā*, *saṅkhārā*, and *viññāṇa*—ignorance, formations ('determinations'), and consciousness. I will show that Ven. Ñāṇavīra's explanations of both these groups of factors fail to draw support from the source that he himself regards as the supreme authority in interpretation of the Dhamma, namely, the Pāli Suttas. I will also show that, contra Ven. Ñāṇavīra, on both points the Suttas confirm the traditional interpretation, which regards these connections as involving a succession of lives.

Let us first turn to Ven. Ñāṇavīra's treatment of the former nexus (§10 of his Note):

> The fundamental *upādāna* or 'holding' is *attavāda*, which is holding a belief in 'self'. The *puthujjana* takes what appears to be his 'self' at its face value; and so long as this goes on he continues to be a 'self', at least in his own eyes (and in those of others like him). This is *bhava* or 'being'. The *puthujjana* knows that people are born and die; and since he thinks 'my self exists' so he also thinks 'my self was born' and 'my self will die'. The *puthujjana* sees a 'self' to whom the words birth and death apply.

Before we go any further, we should point out that Ven. Ñāṇavīra does not cite any suttas to support his understanding of *bhava*, *jāti*, and *jarāmaraṇa*, and in fact there are no suttas to be found in the Pāli Canon that explain the above terms in this way. Moreover, on Ven. Ñāṇavīra's interpretation it may not even be quite correct to say '*jāti-paccayā jarāmaraṇaṃ*'. On his view, it seems, one would be obliged to say instead, '*bhavapaccayā jāti*, *bhavapaccayā jarāmaraṇaṃ*'. Since he regards the *puthujjana*'s taking himself to be a self as the basis for his notions "my self was born" and "my self will die," it would follow that 'being' would be the condition for both 'birth' and 'aging-and-death'. But that is not what the Buddha himself asserts.

In many suttas dealing with PS the Buddha defines the above terms of the formula, and if we look at these texts we will see that they are starkly different from Ven. Ñāṇavīra's explanation of them. The definitions are standardized and can be found at DN 22/D II 305; MN 9/M I 49–50; SN 12:2/S II 2–3, etc.:

> "And what, monks, is aging and death? The aging of beings in the various orders of beings, their old age, brokenness of teeth, greyness of hair, wrinkling of skin, decline of life, weakness of faculties—this is called aging. The passing of beings out of the various orders of beings, their passing away, dissolution, disappearance, dying, completion of time, dissolution of the aggregates, laying down of the body—this is called death. So this aging and this death are (together) called aging-and-death.
>
> "And what, monks, is birth? The birth of beings into the various orders of beings, their coming to birth, descent (into a womb), production, manifestation of the aggregates, obtaining the bases for contact—this is called birth."

The above definitions, with their strings of synonyms and concrete imagery, clearly indicate that 'birth' refers to biological birth and 'aging-and-death' to biological aging and biological death—not to the *puthujjana*'s notions "I was born; I will age and die," or "My self was born; my self ages and dies." The textual definitions are perfectly straightforward and unambiguous in meaning, and give no hint that the Buddha had some other idea to convey about the significance of these terms.

## 4. Bhava and Rebirth

The definition of *bhava* or becoming (Ven. Ñāṇavīra's 'being') offered in the Suttas dealing expressly with PS is nowhere near as transparent as the former definitions, the reason being that the definition of this term is set against the particular cosmology that underlies the Buddha's Teaching. Nevertheless, the Suttas provide no basis for Ven. Ñāṇavīra's claim that *bhava* means the *puthujjana*'s taking himself to be a self.

In the suttas on PS, when the Buddha defines *bhava*, he does so merely by enumerating the three types of becoming:

"And what, monks, is becoming? There are these three types of becoming: sense-sphere becoming; fine-material-sphere becoming; immaterial-sphere becoming."

This definition refers to the three planes of existence in the Buddhist cosmos, and the term '*bhava*' thus would signify concrete individual existence in one or another of these three planes. For illumination as to how *bhava* functions in the PS series, our most helpful resource is the Bhava-sutta, a short exchange between the Buddha and the Venerable Ānanda (AN 3:76/A I 223–24):

"It is said, lord, 'becoming, becoming.' In what way, lord, is there becoming?"

"If, Ānanda, there were no *kamma* ripening in the sense realm, would sense-sphere becoming be discerned?"

"No, lord."

"Thus, Ānanda, *kamma* is the field, consciousness is the seed, craving the moisture; for beings obstructed by ignorance and fettered to craving, consciousness becomes grounded in a low realm. Thus, Ānanda, there is the production of re-becoming in the future. It is thus, Ānanda, that there is becoming.

"If, Ānanda, there were no *kamma* ripening in the fine-material realm, would fine-material becoming be discerned?"

"No, lord."

"Thus, Ānanda, *kamma* is the field, consciousness is the seed, craving the moisture; for beings obstructed by ignorance and fettered to craving, consciousness becomes grounded in a middling realm. Thus, Ānanda, there is the production of re-becoming in the future. It is thus, Ānanda, that there is becoming.

"If, Ānanda, there were no *kamma* ripening in the immaterial realm, would immaterial becoming be discerned?"

"No, lord."

"Thus, Ānanda, *kamma* is the field, consciousness is the seed, craving the moisture; for beings obstructed by ignorance and fettered to craving, consciousness becomes grounded in a superior realm. Thus, Ānanda, there is the production of re-becoming in the future. It is thus, Ānanda, that there is becoming."

Clearly, this sutta is offering a succinct statement of the same basic process described more extensively in the usual twelve-factored formula of *paṭicca-samuppāda*: When there is *avijjā* and *taṇhā*, ignorance and craving, then *kamma*—the volitional action of a being—effects the production of a new existence or 're-becoming in the future' (*āyatiṃ punabbhava*) in a realm that corresponds to the qualitative potential of that *kamma*. It is for this reason that the Commentaries interpret *bhava* in the usual PS formula as having two aspects that pertain to two different lives: one aspect called *kammabhava*, 'kammically active existence', which refers to the *kamma* with the potential of generating rebirth in one or another of the three realms; the other aspect called upapatti*bhava*, 'rebirth existence', which refers to existence produced in one or another of the three realms. Although such a distinction is not explicitly drawn in the old Suttas, it seems to be implied by such passages as the one just quoted above.

Ven. Ñāṇavīra claims that *jāti* does not mean rebirth (§ 9), and he is correct in so far as the word '*jāti*' does not by itself convey the sense of 're-birth'. Nevertheless, within the context of PS (and elsewhere in the Buddha's Teaching), *jāti* must be understood as implying rebirth. In so far as *jāti*, "the manifestation of the aggregates," etc., results from the formation of a new *bhava* "in the future" by the *avijjā*, *taṇhā*, and *kamma* of the preceding existence, any instance of *jāti* is invariably a rebirth of the same continuum of consciousness: the stream of consciousness of the preceding life, "grounded" in a particular realm by reason of its *kamma*, springs up in that realm and comes to growth and full manifestation there.

Contrary to Ven. Ñāṇavīra, throughout the suttas we often find the word '*jāti*' used in conjunction with the terms '*saṃsāra*' and '*punabbhava*' to underscore the fact that rebirth is intended. Take for instance the Buddha's famous "Hymn of Victory" from the Dhammapada (v. 153):

> "I wandered on pointlessly in this cycle
> (*saṃsāra*) of many births
> Seeking the house-builder.
> Painful is birth again and again."
>
> *Anekajātisaṃsāraṃ sandhāvissaṃ anibbisaṃ*
> *Gahakārakaṃ gavesanto dukkhā jāti punappunaṃ.*

Or: "A bhikkhu has abandoned the cycle of births with its re-becoming" (*bhikkhuno ponobhaviko jātisaṃsāro pahīno*; MN 22/M I 139). Or the verse of Udāna 4:9:

"For the monk with a peaceful mind,
When he has cut off craving for becoming,
The wandering on in births is destroyed:
For him there is no re-becoming."

*Ucchinnabhavataṇhassa santacittassa bhikkhuno*
*Vikkhīṇo jātisaṃsāro natthi tassa punabbhavo.*

Again, consider the declaration of final knowledge uttered by the arahants: "This is my last birth; now there is no re-becoming" (*ayam antimā jāti, natthi dāni punabbhavo*; MN 26/M I 167, 173).

The above passages will show us, moreover, that the wedge that Ven. Ñāṇavīra tries to drive between *jāti* and *punabbhavā-bhinibbatti* (in § 10) is a spurious one. While in some passages the two are set in a conditional relationship to one another (the latter being a condition for the former—see S II 65), they are so closely connected that their meanings almost overlap. In fact, the word '*abhinibbatti*' is used as one of the synonyms of *jāti* in the standard definition of the latter. Apparently, when *abhinibbatti* is included in *jāti* we should understand *jāti* as comprising both conception and physical birth, while when they are differentiated, *abhinibbatti* means conception and *jāti* is restricted to full emergence from the womb.

Now that we have adduced textual definitions of the terms 'aging and death', 'birth', and 'becoming', let us see how they link up in the formula of *paṭicca-samuppāda*, as explained by the Buddha himself. The text which elucidates this matter most succinctly is the Mahānidāna-sutta (DN 15/D II 57–58). To bring out the meaning I quote the relevant passage slightly simplified, without the catechistic format, and with the sequence of conditions stated in direct order rather than in reverse order:

"If there were absolutely no clinging of any kind—no clinging to sense pleasures, clinging to views, clinging to rules and observances, clinging to a doctrine of self—then, in the complete absence of clinging, becoming would not be discerned: thus clinging is the condition for becoming.

"If there were absolutely no becoming of any kind—no sense-sphere becoming, fine-material becoming, immaterial becoming—then, in the complete absence of becoming, birth would not be discerned: thus becoming is the condition for birth.

"If there were absolutely no birth of any kind—that is, of gods into the state of gods, of celestials into the state of celestials, of spirits, demons, humans, animals, birds, and reptiles each into their own state—then, in the complete absence of birth, aging and death would not be discerned: thus birth is the condition for aging and death."

Ven. Ñāṇavīra would read this passage to mean: Because the *puthujjana* clings to a belief in self, he goes on being a self (of one or another of the three types); and because he assumes that he is such a self, he thinks "my self was born" and "my self will grow old and die" (see Note, § 10). If, however, we read this passage in the light of the definitions of birth, aging, and death found in the Suttas, and in the light of the Bhava-sutta (AN 3:76), a very different meaning would emerge, which might be formulated thus: Because of clinging of any kind (not only clinging to a doctrine of self), one engages in actions that have the potential to ripen in one or another of the three realms of becoming. These actions dispose consciousness towards these realms. At death, if clinging persists, the predominant *kamma* steers consciousness towards the appropriate realm, i.e. it grounds the "seed" of consciousness in that realm, and thereby generates a new existence. This "production of re-becoming" comes to fulfillment in birth—that is, birth into one of the numerous classes of beings distributed among the three realms of becoming—and once birth occurs, it is inevitably followed by aging and death.

## 5. Three Types of Saṅkhārā

Now let us turn to the other major "plank" in Ven. Ñāṇavīra's *Note on Paṭiccasamuppāda*, his treatment of the interconnections between *avijjā*, *saṅkhārā*, and *viññāṇa* (§§5–6, 11–16). In §5 Ven. Ñāṇavīra cites the threefold enumeration of *saṅkhārā* commonly employed by the Suttas when they analyze the individual factors of the PS formula:

"And what, monks, are the *saṅkhārā*? There are these three *saṅkhārā*: body-*saṅkhāra*, speech-*saṅkhāra*, mind-*saṅkhāra*. These are called the *saṅkhārā*."

I will leave the word '*saṅkhārā*' untranslated here in order not to prejudice the discussion. Immediately after citing this passage, in order to supply definitions of the three types of *saṅkhārā*, Ven. Ñāṇavīra quotes the Cūḷavedalla-sutta (MN 44/M I 301). This sutta—a discussion between the lay devotee Visākha and his former wife, the arahant bhikkhunī Dhammadinnā—defines three types of *saṅkhārā* bearing exactly the same names as those mentioned in the texts on *paṭicca-samuppāda*:

"And which, lady, is body-*saṅkhāra*, which is speech-*saṅkhāra*, which is mind-*saṅkhāra*?"

"The in-&-out breaths are body-*saṅkhāra*, thinking-&-pondering are speech-*saṅkhāra*, perception and feeling are mind-*saṅkhāra*."

Having juxtaposed the two quotations, Ven. Ñāṇavīra then criticizes the traditional interpretation for maintaining that *saṅkhārā* in the PS formula must always be understood as *cetanā* or volition. To make this claim, he asserts, is to wind up holding that the in-&-out breaths, thinking-&-pondering, and perception and feeling, are respectively bodily, verbal, and mental volition—a position that is clearly untenable.

Now both quotations cited above, taken in isolation, are perfectly legitimate. This, however, does not establish that the latter quotation is providing a definition of the same terms intended by the former quotation. While the two triads are expressed in Pāli by the same three compounds—*kāyasaṅkhāra*, *vacīsaṅkhāra*, *cittasaṅkhāra*—Ven. Ñāṇavīra overlooks a fact of prime importance for determining their meaning: namely, that in the Suttas the contexts in which the two triads appear are always kept rigorously separate. The definition of the three *saṅkhārā* found in the Cūḷavedalla Sutta, and elsewhere in the Canon (at S IV 293), does not occur in the context of PS nor in a context that even touches on PS. This particular definition of the three types of *saṅkhārā*—*kāyasaṅkhāra*, *vacīsaṅkhāra*, *cittasaṅkhāra*—always occurs in the course of a discussion on the attainment of the cessation of perception and feeling (*saññāvedayita-nirodha*). It is intended to prepare the way for an explanation of the order in which the three types of *saṅkhārā* cease when a monk enters the attainment of cessation.

But that is not all. Not only are the three *saṅkhārā* of the Cūḷavedalla-sutta always rigorously excluded from discussions of *paṭicca-samuppāda*, but among all the suttas in which the Buddha exemplifies the expressions '*avijjāpaccayā saṅkhārā*' ("with ignorance as condition, formations") and '*saṅkhārapaccayā viññāṇaṃ*' ("with formations as condition, consciousness"), there is not a single text in which he explains *saṅkhārā* in a way that has any relevance to the three kinds of *saṅkhārā* of the Cūḷavedalla Sutta. The two types of discussions of *saṅkhārā*—the threefold enumeration of the Cūḷavedalla-sutta and the threefold enumeration in the PS context—though employing the same terms, are assigned to completely separate compartments. Nowhere in the Sutta-piṭaka does the one triad extend beyond its own context and bear any explicit relationship to the other context. If the Buddha had intended the *saṅkhārā* that are conditioned by ignorance and that condition consciousness to signify the in-&-out breaths, thinking-&-pondering, and perception and feeling, then one could reasonably expect to find at least one sutta on *paṭicca-samuppāda* where he exemplifies *saṅkhārā* by way of the Cūḷavedalla triad. But not a single sutta of such a nature can be found anywhere in the entire Pāli Canon.

Lack of textual corroboration is only one problem with Ven. Ñāṇavīra's proposal to read the Cūḷavedalla triad of *saṅkhārā* into the interpretation of the PS formula. Another objection, even more formidable, can be brought against this suggestion, namely, that it leads to incoherence. For the *saṅkhārā* of the PS formula must be dependent upon ignorance as their necessary condition and must cease with the cessation of ignorance, but the three *saṅkhārā* of the Cūḷavedalla-sutta do not meet this requirement. These *saṅkhārā* are not necessarily dependent upon ignorance and do not cease with the ceasing of ignorance. Though the arahant has completely eradicated ignorance, he continues to breathe in and out (except when in the fourth *jhāna* and higher attainments), to think and ponder (except when in the second and higher *jhāna*s), and to perceive and feel (except when in the cessation of perception and feeling). But what does cease for the arahant with the cessation of ignorance are volitional formations—*saṅkhārā* understood as *sañcetanā*. Whereas the non-arahant's bodily, verbal, and mental activities are constructive forces conditioned by ignorance that sustain the round of rebirths, the arahant's activities are kammically extinct. They no longer sustain the continuation of the round, no longer project consciousness into any new mode of becoming.

In analyzing the teaching of *paṭicca-samuppāda*, the texts use the two terms *cittasaṅkhārā* and *manosaṅkhārā* as though they were interchangeable. This is not typical of the Suttas, which usually reserve *citta* and *mano* for separate contexts. When the texts define *saṅkhārā* in the PS formula, they do so by enumerating the three types of *saṅkhārā*: *kāyasaṅkhāra*, *vacīsaṅkhāra*, *cittasaṅkhāra*; yet they do not take the further step of defining these terms as such. Then, when they exemplify the function of *saṅkhārā* in PS, they employ the triad of *kāyasaṅkhāra*, *vacīsaṅkhāra*, *manosaṅkhāra*. The Pāli Commentaries identify the two triads, taking them as alternative expressions for the same thing; both are understood to refer to bodily volition, verbal volition, and mental volition (*kāyasañcetanā*, *vacīsañcetanā*, *manosañcetanā*). Ven. Ñāṇavīra takes issue with this identification, holding that the two triads must be distinguished. He admits that the second triad is to be identified with *cetanā*, but he insists that the terms used in the first triad have to be understood by way of the explanation given in the Cūḷavedalla Sutta.

This assertion, as we have seen, does not receive confirmation from the Suttas. The original source on which the Pāli Commentaries base their identification of the two triads is the Vibhaṅga of the Abhidhamma-piṭaka. In that work, in the Suttanta-bhājanīya (Sutta Analysis) section of its Paṭicca-samuppāda-vibhaṅga (Vibh 135), we read:

> What are the *saṅkhārā* that are conditioned by ignorance? Meritorious *saṅkhāra*, demeritorious *saṅkhāra*, imperturbable *saṅkhāra*; body-*saṅkhāra*, speech-*saṅkhāra*, mind-*saṅkhāra*....
>
> Therein, bodily volition is body-*saṅkhāra*; verbal volition is speech-*saṅkhāra*, mental volition is mind-*saṅkhāra* (*cittasaṅkhāra*). These are called the *saṅkhārā* conditioned by ignorance.

Ven. Ñāṇavīra may refuse to acknowledge the authority of the Vibhaṅga and insist that he will not relinquish his view unless a sutta can be brought forward confirming this definition. This attitude, however, would appear to be an unreasonable one. Even though the more elaborate conceptions of Abhidhamma thought may be products of a later age than the Suttas, the Suttanta Bhājanīya sections of the Vibhaṅga can make a cogent claim to antiquity. Evidence suggests that this portion of the Vibhaṅga is extremely old, dating from perhaps the third century BC, and thus represents the understanding of the Buddhist community from a period not long after the Buddha's Parinibbāna. It would even be plausible to maintain that this body of material was originally an old commentary on basic Suttanta terminology going back to the very first generation of the Buddha's disciples; it is not specifically Abhidhammic in character and may have been absorbed into the Abhidhamma-piṭaka owing to the lack of any other suitable repository for it.

In any case, in the absence of direct clarification of the issue in the Suttas themselves, the Vibhaṅga becomes the most ancient source to which we can turn for help in clarifying PS terminology. There we find the triad of *kāyasaṅkhāra*, *vacīsaṅkhāra*, and *cittasaṅkhāra* explained in a way that confirms the exclusive identification of the *saṅkhārā* factor in the PS formula with *cetanā*. This lends weight to the view that this second link should be taken as *kamma* and its relation to *viññāṇa* as that of the kammic cause from the preceding existence.

## 6. The Meaning of 'saṅkhārā'

I intend to examine very briefly all the suttas that help shed light on the *saṅkhārā* factor in PS formulation, as found in the Nidāna-saṃyutta, the Buddha's collected short discourses on dependent arising. But first a few words should be said about Ven. Ñāṇavīra's general understanding of the word '*saṅkhārā*'. Ven. Ñāṇavīra maintains that this word has a univocal meaning relevant to all the contexts in which it occurs. The meaning he assigns to it is that of "something upon which something else depends"(§ 11); hence his rendering 'determinations'. The Suttas themselves do not offer a single etymological derivation of the word with unrestricted application. The well-known derivation—*saṅkhataṃ abhisaṅkharontī ti tasmā saṅkhārā ti vuccanti* (in Ven. Ñāṇavīra's terminology, "They determine the determined, therefore they are called determinations")—applies specifically to *saṅkhārā* as the fourth of the five aggregates, not to *saṅkhārā* in all usages. In this context they obviously signify *cetanā*, volition, understood as a constructive force, and thus an active derivation is appropriate.

The Pāli Commentaries offer two derivations of the word '*saṅkhārā*'. One is active (as given above), the other passive (*saṅkharīyantī ti saṅkhārā*). Thus the Commentaries hold that the word can signify either things that actively produce other things, or things that are produced by other things. Which meaning is relevant depends on the context. In the two contexts of *paṭicca-samuppāda* and the fourth aggregate, the active sense is relevant, as in both cases the *saṅkhārā* are volitions. But in such statements as '*sabbe saṅkhārā aniccā*', etc., the Commentaries explain that *saṅkhārā* should be understood as *saṅkhata-saṅkhārā*, that is, as conditioned things.

According to the Majjhima-nikāya Commentary, the passive sense also pertains to two of the three *saṅkhārā* of the Cūḷavedalla-sutta: (i) the in-&-out breaths are body-*saṅkhāra* because they are determined by the body, made by the body, produced by the body; (iii) perception and feeling are mind-*saṅkhāra* because they are determined by the mind, made by the mind, produced by the mind. In contrast, (ii) thinking-&-pondering, as speech-*saṅkhāra*, play an active role: they are determinants of speech.

The commentarial recognition of a twofold derivation of the term '*saṅkhārā*' seems to be confirmed by the texts. For instance, the Cūḷavedalla-sutta explains:

> "In-&-out breaths, friend Visākha, are bodily, these things are dependent upon the body; that is why the in-&-out breaths are the body-*saṅkhāra*.... Perception and feeling are mental, these things are dependent upon the mind; that is why perception and feeling are mind-*saṅkhāra*."

In contrast, Ven. Ñāṇavīra's insistence on assigning an exclusively active sense to *saṅkhārā* compels him to apply the old Procrustean bed of exegesis to several passages that do not easily submit to his interpretation. For example, in his separate note on *Saṅkhāra*, he attempts to explain how the reference to *saṅkhārā* in the Mahāsudassana Suttanta (DN 17/D II 169ff.) can be interpreted in line with his view of *saṅkhārā* as active determinations. In this sutta the Buddha, after describing all the rich endowments and possessions of King Mahāsudassana, a king of the distant past, concludes with a homily on impermanence: "See, Ānanda, how all those *saṅkhārā* have passed, ceased, altered. So impermanent, Ānanda, are *saṅkhārā* ... this is enough for weariness with all *saṅkhārā*, enough for dispassion, enough for release." Ven. Ñāṇavīra discerns a cryptic message concealed in this passage thus: "Those things [the possessions, etc.] were *saṅkhārā*; they were things on which King Mahāsudassana depended for his very identity; they determined his person as 'King Mahāsudassana', and with their cessation the thought 'I am King Mahāsudassana' came to an end." There is nothing in the sutta itself to support this interpretation, and the text (as well as others of a similar character) reads so much more naturally if we take *saṅkhārā* simply to mean the conditioned things of the world. Moreover, other suttas can be found which include the same final exhortation on dispassion, yet which provide absolutely no ground for seeing the term *saṅkhārā* there as determinants of anyone's personal identity (see e.g. the Anamatagga-saṃyutta, SN 15/S II 178ff.).

## 7. Saṅkhārā in the PS Formula

Let us now turn directly to the Nidāna-saṃyutta to see how the suttas on *paṭicca-samuppāda* treat the term '*saṅkhārā*' in relation to *avijjā* and *viññāṇa*. As the suttas in this collection that expand upon the stock formula are conveniently few in number, we can take a brief look at each in turn. Of these texts, two establish the two major paradigms for the interpretation of *saṅkhārā*, namely, that formulated in terms of the three doors of volitional action and that formulated in terms of three kammically graded types of volition. Besides these, three additional texts can be found that shed light on the problem. I should stress at once that the Nidāna-saṃyutta incorporates virtually all the shorter discourses of the Buddha dealing with *paṭicca-samuppāda*, and hence should be taken as definitive in its presentation of the meaning and function of the constituent items in the formula.

We will begin with the Bhūmija Sutta, the paradigmatic text for distinguishing *saṅkhārā* by way of the doors of action:

> "When there is the body, Ānanda, because of bodily volition there arises internally pleasure and pain. When there is speech, because of verbal volition there arises internally pleasure and pain. When there is the mind, because of mental volition there arises internally pleasure and pain.

"With ignorance as condition, either by oneself, Ānanda, one forms that body-*saṅkhāra* (speech-*saṅkhāra*, mind-*saṅkhāra*) on account of which that pleasure and pain arises internally; or because of others one forms that body-*saṅkhāra* (speech-*saṅkhāra*, mind-*saṅkhāra*) on account of which that pleasure and pain arises internally...

"Ignorance is included among these things. But with the remainderless fading away and cessation of ignorance that body does not exist (that speech does not exist, that mind does not exist) on account of which that pleasure and pain arises internally."

Here the three *saṅkhārā* that are said to be conditioned by ignorance are explicitly identified with the three types of volition. The sutta employs the term '*manosaṅkhāra*' rather than '*cittasaṅkhāra*', but in the absence of any other exemplification of *cittasaṅkhāra* in the PS context, we can take the terms as interchangeable; though such usage is not common, it is not totally foreign to the Nikāyas and other instances can be cited of the synonymous use of *citta* and *mano*.

According to the commentary, this volition is to be understood as *kamma*, and the pleasure and pain that arise internally as *vipāka-vedanā*, as feelings resulting from that *kamma*. A temporal separation between the volition and the resulting pleasure and pain may not be explicitly mentioned in the text, but if we read the above passage against the broader background of the Suttas, we can readily infer that an implicit temporal gap is intended. One sutta in the Aṅguttara-nikāya, on the correlations between *kamma* and its fruit, helps us to understand the process by which *saṅkhārā* function as conditions for the arising of pleasant and painful feeling:

Here, monks, someone forms an afflictive body-*saṅkhāra*, speech-*saṅkhāra*, mind-*saṅkhāra*. Having done so, he is reborn into an afflictive world. When he is reborn there afflictive contacts contact him, and he experiences feelings that are extremely painful.... Someone forms a non-afflictive body-*saṅkhāra*, (etc.) ... he is reborn into a non-afflictive world.... Non-afflictive contacts contact him, and he experiences feelings that are extremely pleasant.... Someone forms both an afflictive and a non-afflictive body-*saṅkhāra*, (etc.) ... he is reborn into a world that is both afflictive and non-afflictive. Afflictive and non-afflictive contacts contact him, and he experiences feelings that are both painful and pleasant."

Here the term used is again '*manosaṅkhāra*', and it is clear that the three *saṅkhārā* are primarily of interest because they determine a person's plane of rebirth and the quality of affective experience prevailing in his life. The sutta is not manifestly concerned with PS, but if we examine the sequence of events being described we would find, embedded in it, a segment of the standard PS formula. These events can be represented thus: *saṅkhārā* > rebirth into a world > contact > feeling. From the Mahānidāna-sutta (DN 15/D II 63) we know that rebirth into any world involves the co-arising of consciousness and name-and-form, and from the latter we can elicit the six sense bases as the condition for contact. This suffices to establish that the above text and the PS formula are defining the same situation, and here it is evident that the *saṅkhārā* serve as condition for the arising of pleasure and pain across the gap of lifetimes.

The last paragraph of the above quotation from the Bhūmija-sutta expresses obliquely the converse side of the relationship. Here, when the Buddha states that with the cessation of ignorance, body, speech, and mind no longer serve as conditions for pleasure and pain to arise internally, what is meant is that these doors of action cease to be instruments for generating *saṅkhārā*, actions with the power to produce re-becoming. When ignorance is eliminated, volition no longer functions as *saṅkhārā*, as a constructive power that builds up new edifices of personal existence in future lives. The actions of the arahant, whether performed by body, speech, or mind, are *khīṇabīja*, "with seed destroyed" (Ratana-sutta, Sn 235); they are incapable of ripening in the future, and hence no longer serve as conditions for pleasure and pain to arise.

The second major paradigm for understanding the *saṅkhārā* factor in PS, and its relations to *avijjā* and *viññāṇa*, grades the *saṅkhārā* according to their ethical quality, which in turn indicates the type of rebirth they produce. This paradigm is delineated in the following passage:

"Bhikkhus, if a person immersed in ignorance forms a meritorious *saṅkhāra*, consciousness goes on towards merit. If he forms a demeritorious *saṅkhāra*, consciousness goes on towards demerit. If he forms an imperturbable *saṅkhāra*, consciousness goes on towards the imperturbable."

Once again it is obvious that we must understand *saṅkhārā* as volition (*cetanā*). And once again it is not so obvious that the relationship between *saṅkhārā* and consciousness may be a causal one operating across different lives. The commentary to the sutta explains that the phrase "consciousness goes on towards merit" can be understood in two complementary ways: (i) the kammically active consciousness associated with the volition "goes on towards" meritorious *kamma*, i.e. it accumulates merit; and (ii) the consciousness resulting from the merit "goes on towards" the result of merit, i.e. it reaps the fruits of that merit. The same principle of interpretation applies to the other two cases—the demeritorious and the imperturbable. Thus the point of the passage, as understood from the traditional perspective, may be paraphrased thus: A meritorious volition infuses consciousness with a meritorious quality and thereby steers consciousness towards rebirth in a realm resulting from merit; a demeritorious volition infuses consciousness with a demeritorious quality and thereby steers consciousness towards rebirth in a realm resulting from demerit; an imperturbable volition infuses consciousness with an imperturbable quality (*āneñja*) and thereby steers consciousness towards rebirth in an imperturbable realm, i.e. a realm corresponding to the fourth *jhāna* or the formless meditative attainments.

Ven. Ñāṇavīra himself rejects this interpretation of the passage. He writes (§ 15):

> ... Nothing in the Sutta suggests that *puññūpagaviññāṇa* is anything other than the meritorious consciousness of one who is determining or intending merit. (When merit is intended by an individual he is conscious of his world as 'world-for-doing-merit-in', and consciousness has thus 'arrived at merit'.)

My reading of the passage disagrees with that of Ven. Ñāṇavīra. Even if we disregard the commentarial explanation sketched above and focus solely on the text, we would find that the structure of the sutta itself suggests that a *kamma-vipāka* relationship is intended by the link between *saṅkhārā* and *viññāṇa*. For the sutta continues: When a bhikkhu has abandoned ignorance and aroused knowledge, he does not form any of the three types of *saṅkhārā*. Thereby he reaches arahantship, and when his body breaks up with the ending of his life, he attains Parinibbāna. Thus "all that is felt, not being delighted in, will become cool right here, and bodily elements only will remain." Hence, in its structure, the sutta establishes a contrast between the ignorant worldling and the arahant. The worldling, by fashioning meritorious, demeritorious, and imperturbable volitions, projects his consciousness into a new existence, setting in motion once again the entire cycle of birth and death. The arahant cuts off ignorance and stops forming *saṅkhārā*, thus ending the grounding of consciousness and the consequent renewal of the cycle.

This conclusion can draw further support from a study of how the word '*upaga*' is used in the Suttas. Ven. Ñāṇavīra's rendering "has arrived at" is actually an error: the word functions not as a past participle (that would be *upagata*) but as a suffix signifying present action. Hence I render it "goes on towards." In contexts similar to the one cited above (though perhaps not in all contexts) '*upaga*' most commonly denotes movement towards the fruition of one's past *kamma*—movement fulfilled by the process of rebirth. Consider the stock passage on the exercise of the divine eye:

> "With the divine eye, which is purified and superhuman, he sees beings passing away and being reborn, inferior and superior, beautiful and ugly, fortunate and unfortunate, and he understands how beings go on in accordance with their *kamma*."

Then consider the Āneñjasappāya-sutta, on a bhikkhu who practises the "imperturbable meditations" without reaching arahantship: "With the breakup of the body, after death, it is possible that his consciousness, evolving on, may go on towards the imperturbable." Note that the last expression (*viññāṇaṃ āneñjūpagaṃ*), in the Pāli, is identical with the expression found in the Nidāna-saṃyutta sutta cited above, and here, clearly, a transition from one life to another is involved.

We thus see that in the two main models for the *saṅkhārā* factor of PS presented by the Nidāna-saṃyutta, the term signifies volitional activity, and its bearing on consciousness and feeling is that of kammic cause for a fruit generally maturing in a subsequent life. We should further stress that these two models are neither mutually exclusive nor do they concern different material. Rather, they structure the same material—kammically potent volitions—along different lines, depending on the perspective adopted, whether the perspective of door of action or that of ethical quality.

Besides these two major models, the Nidāna-saṃyutta contains two short suttas that help illuminate the role of *saṅkhārā* in the PS formula. We may begin with the following:

> "Bhikkhus, if there is lust, delight, craving for solid food (or any of the other three types of nutriment), consciousness becomes grounded in that and comes to growth. When consciousness is grounded and comes to growth, there is a descent of name-and-form. When there is a descent of name-and-form, there is the growth of *saṅkhārā*. When there is the growth of *saṅkhārā*, there is the production of re-becoming in the future. When there is the production of re-becoming in the future, there is future birth, aging and death."

Here we can see that *saṅkhārā* are responsible for bringing about "re-becoming in the future," that is, for generating rebirth. The structure of the sutta is similar to that of the Bhava-sutta quoted above (AN 3:76), but here three existences are implied. The first is the existence in which there is craving for food. This craving, accompanied by ignorance, grounds consciousness in its attachment to nutriment. Consciousness—here the kammically active consciousness—is the seed arisen in the old existence that sprouts forth as a new existence, causing a "descent" of name-and-form into the womb. Within that second existence the new being, on reaching maturity, engages in volitional activity, which brings on "the growth of *saṅkhārā*." These *saṅkhārā* in turn, enveloped by ignorance and craving, initiate the production of still another existence, the third of the series. This existence (like all others) commences with birth and terminates in aging and death.

Next, let us look at one short sutta in the Nidāna-saṃyutta which explicitly mentions neither *avijjā* nor *saṅkhārā* but refers to them obliquely:

> "What one wills, and what one plans, and what lies latent within—this is a support for the continuance of consciousness. When there is a support, there is a grounding of consciousness. When consciousness is grounded and comes to growth, there is the production of re-becoming in the future. When there is the production of re-becoming in the future, future birth, aging and

death, sorrow, lamentation, pain, displeasure, and despair arise. Such is the origin of this whole mass of suffering."

In this sutta, *saṅkhārā* are referred to elliptically by the expressions '*yaṃ ceteti*', "what one wills," and '*yaṃ pakappeti*', "what one plans" ('*pakappeti*' is a rare term, apparently synonymous with '*ceteti*'). The expression '*yaṃ anuseti*', "what lies latent within," points to the *anusaya*, the latent tendencies, which other texts tell us include the latent tendency of ignorance (*avijjānusaya*) and the latent tendency of lust or craving (*rāgānusaya*). Thus the sutta is stating that when one forms volitions on the basis of ignorance and craving, these volitions become a support which grounds consciousness and establishes it in a new existence. Once consciousness becomes so established, it sets in motion the entire production of the new existence, beginning with birth and ending with death, accompanied by all its attendant suffering.

The text which immediately follows the afore mentioned sutta in the Nidāna-saṃyutta (SN 12:39), begins identically as far as "and comes to growth," then it continues with "there is a descent of name-and-form" and the rest of the standard series. This shows that in the PS context "the descent of name-and-form" (*nāmarūpassa avakkanti*) is effectively synonymous with "the production of re-becoming in the future" (*āyatiṃ punabbhavābhinibbatti*). Both signify the unfolding of the rebirth process once consciousness has gained a foothold in the new existence.

The above analysis should be sufficient to establish with reasonable certainty that the term '*saṅkhārā*' in the PS formula denotes nothing other than volition (*cetanā*), and that volition enters into the formula because it is the factor primarily responsible for "grounding" consciousness in the round of repeated becoming and for driving it into a new form of existence in the future. When this much is recognized, it becomes unnecessary for me to say anything about the continuation of Ven. Ñāṇavīra's Note on PS from § 18 to the end. This convoluted discussion rests upon Ven. Ñāṇavīra's assumption that the term '*saṅkhārā*' in the PS formula comprises all the varieties of *saṅkhārā* spoken of in the Suttas, that is, all things that other things depend on. By adopting this thesis Ven. Ñāṇavīra finds himself obliged to explain how such things as the in-&-out breaths, etc., can be said to be conditioned by ignorance and to be conditions for consciousness. The explanation he devises may be ingenious, but as it receives no confirmation from the Suttas themselves, we can conclude that his account does not correctly represent the Buddha's intention in expounding the teaching of *paṭicca-samuppāda.*

At this point we can pull together the main threads of our discussion. We have seen that the alternative, "more satisfactory approach" to *paṭicca-samuppāda* that Ven. Ñāṇavīra proposes rests on two planks: one is his interpretation of the nexus of *bhava*, *jāti*, and *jarāmaraṇa*, the other his interpretation of the nexus of *avijjā*, *saṅkhārā*, and *viññāṇa*. The first hinges on ascribing to all three terms meanings that cannot be substantiated by the texts. The second involves a merging of two contexts that the texts rigorously keep separate, namely, the PS context and the definition of the three *saṅkhārā* stated in connection with the attainment of the cessation of perception and feeling (found in the Cūḷavedalla-sutta). This error leads Ven. Ñāṇavīra to assign to the term '*saṅkhārā*' in the PS context a much wider meaning than the texts allow. It also induces him to overlook the various passages from the Suttas that clearly show that *saṅkhārā* in the PS formula must always be understood as volitional activities, considered principally by way of their role in projecting consciousness into a new existence in the future.

To round off this portion of my critique, I would like to take a quick look at a short sutta in the Nidāna-saṃyutta—a terse and syntactically tricky text—that confirms the three-life interpretation of PS almost as explicitly as one might wish. Our text—the Bālapaṇḍita-sutta (SN 12:19/S II 23–24)—opens thus:

> "Bhikkhus, for the fool, hindered by ignorance and fettered by craving, this body has thereby been obtained. Hence there is this body and external name-and-form: thus this dyad. Dependent on the dyad there is contact. There are just six sense bases, contacted through which—or through a certain one of them—the fool experiences pleasure and pain."

Exactly the same thing is said regarding the wise man. The Buddha then asks the monks to state the difference between the two, and when the monks defer, the Master continues:

> "For the fool, hindered by ignorance and fettered by craving, this body has been obtained. But for the fool that ignorance has not been abandoned and that craving has not been eliminated.

Why not? Because the fool has not lived the holy life for the complete destruction of suffering. Therefore, with the breakup of the body, the fool is one who goes on to (another) body. Being one who goes onto (another) body, he is not freed from birth, from aging and death, not freed from sorrow, lamentation, pain, grief, despair; he is not freed from suffering, I say."

The wise man, in contrast, having lived the holy life to the full, has abandoned ignorance and eliminated craving. Thus with the breakup of the body, he is not one who goes on to another body, and thus he is freed from birth, aging, death, etc.; he is freed from all kinds of suffering.

Having been included in the Nidāna-saṃyutta, this sutta must be an exemplification of PS; otherwise it would have no place in that collection. And we can detect, with minor variants and elisions, the main factors of the classical formula. Yet not only are three lifetimes explicitly depicted, but we also find two other basic exegetical tools of the Commentaries already well adumbrated: the three links (*tisandhi*) and the four groups (*catusaṅkhepa*). The first group—the causal factors of the past life—are the ignorance and craving that brought both the fool and the wise man into the present existence; though *saṅkhārā* are not mentioned, they are implied by the mention of ignorance. The first link—that between past causes and present results—connects past ignorance and craving with "this body." This, obviously, is a conscious body (*saviññāṇaka kāya*), implying *viññāṇa*. The text mentions the remaining factors of the present resultant group: *nāmarūpa*, *saḷāyatana*, *phassa*, *vedanā*. Then, in the case of the fool, a link takes place between the present resultant group—epitomized by the experience of pleasure and pain—and the present causal group productive of a future life. This group is represented by the present *avijjā* and *taṇhā* that the fool has not discarded. We also know, despite the elision, that *taṇhā* will lead to *upādāna* and a fresh surge of volitional activity motivated by clinging (the *kammabhava* of the Commentaries).

Because of his *avijjā* and *taṇhā* the fool "goes on to another body" (*kāyūpago hoti*)—note that here we meet once again the word upaga which I discussed above (§ 15), again in connection with the rebirth process. The "going on to (another) body" can be seen as loosely corresponding to *punabbhavābhinibbatti*, which is followed by birth, aging, and death, etc. These last factors are the fourth group, future effects, linked to the third group, the present-life causes. Thus in this short sutta, which fills out the bare-bones standard formula with some strips of flesh, however lean, we can discern the exegetical tools of the Commentaries already starting to take shape.

## 8. IN DEFENSE OF TRADITION

Now we can return to the opening sections of Ven. Ñāṇavīra's *Note on Paṭiccasamuppāda* and examine his criticisms of the traditional interpretation.

In § 3 Ven. Ñāṇavīra argues against the commentarial view that *vedanā* in the standard PS formula must be restricted to *kammavipāka*. For proof to the contrary he appeals to the Sīvaka-sutta (SN 36:21/S IV 230–31), in which the Buddha mentions eight causes of bodily pain, of which only the last is *kammavipāka*. On the traditional interpretation, Ven. Ñāṇavīra says, this would limit the application of *paṭicca-samuppāda* to certain bodily feelings but would exclude other types of feeling. Such a view, he holds, is contradicted by the Buddha's unrestricted declaration that pleasure and pain are dependently arisen (*paṭicca-samuppannaṃ kho āvuso sukhadukkhaṃ vuttaṃ bhagavatā*; S II 38).

This objection in no way overturns the traditional view of dependent arising. It should first be pointed out that the notion of *paṭicca-samuppāda* has a twofold significance, as Ven. Ñāṇavīra himself recognizes in his Note (§ 18). The notion refers both to a structural principle, i.e. the principle that things arise in dependence on conditions, and it refers to various exemplifications of that structural principle, the most common being the twelvefold formula. Once we call attention to this distinction, the traditional interpretation is easily vindicated: All feelings are dependently arisen in so far as they arise from conditions, principally from contact along with such conditions as sense faculty, object, consciousness, etc. This, however, does not require that all feelings be included in the *vedanā* factor of the standard PS formula. Without violating the structural principle that all feeling is dependently arisen, the Commentaries can consistently confine this factor to the feelings that result from previous *kamma*.

While recognizing that the Pāli Commentaries do restrict *vedanā* in the standard PS formula to *vipākavedanā*, we might suggest another line of interpretation different from the commentarial one, a line which is less narrow yet still respects the view that the PS formula describes a process extending over successive lives. On this view, rather than insist that the *vedanā* link be understood literally and exclusively as specific resultant feelings born of specific past *kamma*, we might instead hold that the *vedanā* link should be understood as the result of past *kamma* only in the more general sense that the capacity for experiencing feeling is a consequence of obtaining a sentient organism through the force of past *kamma*. That is, it is past *kamma*, accompanied by ignorance and craving, that brought into being the present sentient organism equipped with its six sense bases through which feeling is experienced. If this view is adopted, we can hold that the capacity for experiencing feeling—the obtaining of a psycho-physical organism (*nāmarūpa*) with its six sense bases (*saḷāyatana*)—is the product of past *kamma*, but we need not hold that every feeling comprised in the *vedanā* link is the fruit of a particular past *kamma*. The predominant feeling-tone of a given existence will be a direct result of specific *kamma*, but it would not necessarily follow that every passively experienced feeling is actual *vipāka*. This would allow us to include all feeling within the standard PS formula without deviating from the governing principle of the traditional interpretation that the five links, from consciousness through feeling, are fruits of past *kamma*. Although the Commentaries do take the hard line that feeling in the PS formula is *kammavipāka* in the strict sense, this "softer" interpretation is in no way contradicted by the Suttas. Both approaches, however, concur in holding that the five above-mentioned factors in any given life result from the ignorance, craving, and volitional activity of the preceding life.

In the next section (§ 4) Ven. Ñāṇavīra warns us that "there is a more serious difficulty regarding feeling" posed by the traditional interpretation. He refers to a sutta (AN 3:61/A I 176) in which, he says, three types of feeling—*somanassa* (joy), *domanassa* (sadness), and *upekkhā* (equanimity)—"are included in *vedanā*, in the specific context of the PS formulation." These three feelings, he continues, necessarily involve *cetanā*, intention or volition, as intrinsic to their structure, and therefore the Commentary must either exclude them from *vedanā* in the PS formulation or else must regard them as *vipāka*. Both horns of this dilemma, Ven. Ñāṇavīra contends, are untenable: the former, because it contradicts the sutta (which, he says, includes them under *vedanā* in the PS context); the latter, because reflection establishes that these feelings involve *cetanā* and thus cannot be *vipāka*.

The Pāli Commentaries, which adopt the Abhidhamma classification of feeling, hold that *somanassa*, *domanassa*, and *upekkhā*—in the present context—are kammically active rather than resultant feelings. This would exclude them from the *vedanā* factor of the PS formulation, which Ven. Ñāṇavīra claims contradicts the sutta under discussion. But if we turn to the sutta itself, as Ven. Ñāṇavīra himself urges, we will find that the section dealing with these three types of feeling does not have any discoverable connection with *paṭicca-samuppāda*, and it is perplexing why Ven. Ñāṇavīra should assert that it does. *Paṭicca-samuppāda* is introduced later in the sutta, but the section where these three types of feeling are mentioned is not related to any formulation of *paṭicca-samuppāda* at all. The entire passage reads as follows:

> "'These eighteen mental examinations, monks, are the Dhamma taught by me ... not to be denied by wise recluses and brahmins.' Such has been said. And with reference to what was this said? Having seen a form with the eye, one examines a form that is a basis for joy, one examines a form that is a basis for sadness, one examines a form that is a basis for equanimity. (The same is repeated for the other five senses.) It was with reference to this that it was said: 'These eighteen mental examinations, monks, are the Dhamma taught by me ... not to be denied by wise recluses and brahmins.'"

And that is it. Thus "the more serious difficulty regarding feeling" that Ven. Ñāṇavīra sees in the commentarial interpretation turns out to be no difficulty at all, but only his own strangely careless misreading of the passage.

In the same paragraph Ven. Ñāṇavīra derides the commentarial notion that *nāmarūpa* in the PS formulation is *vipāka*. He points out that *nāma* includes *cetanā*, volition or intention, and this leads the Commentary to speak of *vipākacetanā*: "But the Buddha has said (AN 6:63/A III 415) that *kamma* is *cetanā* (action is intention), and the notion of *vipākacetanā*, consequently, is a plain self-contradiction."

Here again the commentarial position can easily be defended. The Buddha's full statement should be considered first:

> "It is volition, monks, that I call *kamma*. Having willed (or intended), one does *kamma* by body, speech, or mind."

The Buddha's utterance does not establish a mathematical equivalence between *cetanā* and *kamma*, such that every instance of volition must be considered *kamma*. As the second part of his statement shows, his words mean that *cetanā* is the decisive factor in action, that which motivates action and confers upon action the ethical significance intrinsic to the idea of *kamma*. This implies that the ethical evaluation of a deed is to be based on the *cetanā* from which it springs, so that a deed has no kammic efficacy apart from the *cetanā* to which it gives expression. The statement does not imply that *cetanā* (in the non-arahant) is always and invariably *kamma*.

In order to see that the notion of *vipākacetanā* is not self-contradictory nor even unintelligible, we need only consider the statements occasionally found in the Suttas about *nāmarūpa* descending into the womb or taking shape in the womb (e.g. DN 15/II 63; also § 17 above). It is undeniable that the *nāmarūpa* that "descends" into the womb is the result of past *kamma*, hence *vipāka*. Yet this *nāma* includes *cetanā*, and hence that *cetanā* too must be *vipāka*. Further, the Suttas establish that *cetanā*, as the chief factor in the fourth aggregate (the *saṅkhārakkhandha*), is present on every occasion of experience. A significant portion of experience is *vipāka*, and thus the *cetanā* intrinsic to this experience must be *vipāka*. When one experiences feeling as the result of past *kamma*, the *cetanā* coexisting with that feeling must be *vipāka* too. The Commentaries squarely confront the problem of *cetanā* in resultant states of consciousness and explain how this *cetanā* can perform the distinct function of *cetanā* without constituting *kamma* in the common sense of that word. (See *Atthasālinī*, pp. 87–88; *The Expositor* (PTS trans.), pp. 116–17.)

# 9. THE PROBLEM OF TIME

The main reason for Ven. Ñāṇavīra's dissatisfaction with the traditional interpretation of *paṭicca-samuppāda* emerges in § 7 of his Note. The traditional view regards the PS formula as describing a sequence spread out over three lives, hence as involving succession in time. For Ven. Ñāṇavīra this view closes off the prospect of an immediate ascertainment that one has reached the end of suffering. He argues that since I cannot see my past life or my future life, the three-life interpretation of PS removes a significant part of the formula from my immediate sphere of vision. Thus *paṭicca-samuppāda* becomes "something that, in part at least, must be taken on trust." But because PS is designed to show the prospect for a present solution to the present problem of existential anxiety, it must describe a situation that pertains entirely to the present. Hence Ven. Ñāṇavīra rejects the view of PS as a description of the rebirth process and instead takes it to define an ever-present existential structure of the unenlightened consciousness.

The examination of the suttas on *paṭicca-samuppāda* that we have undertaken above has confirmed that the usual twelve-term formula applies to a succession of lives. This conclusion must take priority over all deductive arguments against temporal succession in *paṭicca-samuppāda*. The Buddha's Teaching certainly does show us the way to release from existential anxiety. Since such anxiety, or agitation (*paritassanā*), depends upon clinging, and clinging involves the taking of things to be 'mine', 'what I am', and 'my self', the elimination of clinging will bring the eradication of anxiety. The Buddha offers a method of contemplation that focuses on things as anattā, as 'not mine', 'not I', 'not my self'. Realization of the characteristic of anattā removes clinging, and with the elimination of clinging anxiety is removed, including existential anxiety over our inevitable aging and death. This, however, is not the situation being described by the PS formula, and to read the one in terms of the other is to engage in an unjustifiable confounding of distinct frames of reference.

From his criticism of the three-life interpretation of *paṭicca-samuppāda*, it appears that Ven. Ñāṇavīra entertains a mistaken conception of what it would mean to see PS within the framework of three lives. He writes (§ 7):

"Now it is evident that the twelve items, *avijjā* to *jarāmaraṇa*, cannot, if the traditional interpretation is correct, all be seen at once; for they are spread over three successive existences. I may, for example, see present *viññāṇa* to *vedanā*, but I cannot now see the *kamma* of the past existence—*avijjā* and *saṅkhāra*—that (according to the traditional interpretation) was the cause of these present things. Or I may see *taṇhā* and so on, but I cannot now see the *jāti* and *jarāmaraṇa* that will result from these things in the next existence."

In Ven. Ñāṇavīra's view, on the traditional interpretation, in order to see PS properly, I would have to be able to see the *avijjā* and *saṅkhāra* of my past life that brought about this present existence, and I would also have to be able to see the birth, aging, and death I will undergo in a future existence as a result of my present craving. Since such direct perception of the past and future is not, according to the Suttas, an integral part of every noble disciple's range of knowledge, he concludes that the traditional interpretation is unacceptable.

Reflection would show that the consequences that Ven. Ñāṇavīra draws do not necessarily follow from the three-life interpretation. To meet Ven. Ñāṇavīra's argument, let us first remember that the Commentaries do not treat the twelvefold formula of PS as a rigid series whose factors are assigned to tightly segregated time-frames. The formula is regarded, rather, as an expository device spread out over three lives in order to demonstrate the self-sustaining internal dynamics of saṃsāric becoming. The situation defined by the formula is in actuality not a simple linear sequence, but a more complex process by which ignorance, craving, and clinging in unison generate renewed becoming in a direction determined by the *saṅkhāra*, the kammically potent volitional activity. Any new existence begins with the simultaneous arising of *viññāṇa* and *nāmarūpa*, culminating in birth, the full manifestation of the five aggregates. With these aggregates as the basis, ignorance, craving, and clinging, again working in unison, generate a fresh store of *kamma* productive of still another becoming, and so the process goes on until ignorance and craving are eliminated.

Hence to see and understand PS within the framework of the three-life interpretation is not a matter of running back mentally into the past to recollect the specific causes in the past life that brought about present existence, nor of running ahead mentally into the next life to see the future effects of the present causal factors. To see PS effectively is, rather, to see that ignorance, craving, and clinging have the inherent power to generate renewed becoming, and then to understand, on this basis, that present existence must have been brought to pass through the ignorance, craving, and clinging of the past existence, while any uneradicated ignorance, craving, and clinging will bring to pass a new existence in the future. Although the application of the PS formula involves temporal extension over a succession of lives, what one sees with immediate vision is not the connection between particular events in the past, present, and future, but conditional relationships obtaining between types of phenomena: that phenomena of a given type B arise in necessary dependence on phenomena of type A, that phenomena of a given type C arise in necessary dependence on phenomena of type B.

Of these relationships, the most important is the connection between craving and re-becoming. Craving, underlaid by ignorance and fortified by clinging, is the force that originates new existence and thereby keeps the wheel of *saṃsāra* in motion. This is already implied by the stock formula of the second noble truth: "And what, monks, is the origin of suffering? It is craving, which produces re-becoming (*taṇhā ponobhavikā*)...." The essential insight disclosed by the PS formula is that any given state of existence has come to be through prior craving, and that uneradicated craving has the inherent power to generate new becoming. Once this single principle is penetrated, the entire twelvefold series follows as a matter of course.

Ven. Ñāṇavīra implicitly attempts to marshal support for his non-temporal interpretation of PS by quoting as the epigraph to his *Note on Paṭiccasamuppāda* the following excerpt from the Cūḷasakuludāyi Sutta:

> "But, Udāyi, let be the past, let be the future, I shall set you forth the Teaching: 'When there is this, that is; with arising of this, that arises; when there is not this, that is not; with cessation of this, that ceases.'"

Here, apparently, the Buddha proposes the abstract principle of conditionality as an alternative to teachings about temporal matters relating to the past and future. Since in other suttas the statement of the abstract principle is immediately followed by the entire twelve-term formula, the conclusion seems to follow that any application of temporal distinctions to PS, particularly the attempt to see it as extending to the past and future, would be a violation of the Buddha's intention.

This conclusion, however, would be premature, and if we turn to the sutta from which the quotation has been extracted we would see that the conclusion is actually unwarranted. In the sutta the non-Buddhist wanderer Sakuludāyi tells the Buddha that recently one famous teacher had been claiming omniscience, but when he approached this teacher—who turns out to have been the Jain leader Nigaṇṭha Nātaputta—and asked him a question about the past, the teacher had tried to evade the question, to turn the discussion aside, and became angry and resentful. He expresses the trust that the Buddha is skilled in such matters. The Buddha then says: "One who can recollect his previous births back for many aeons might engage with me in a fruitful discussion about matters pertaining to the past, while one who has the knowledge of the passing away and rebirth of beings might engage with me in a fruitful discussion about matters pertaining to the future." Then, since Udāyi has neither such knowledge, at this point the Buddha states: "But, Udāyi, let be the past, let be the future," and he cites the abstract principle of conditionality. Thus the purport of the Buddha's statement, read as a whole, is that without such super-knowledges of the past and the future, there is no point discussing specific empirical factual matters concerning the past and the future. The Buddha's dismissal of these issues by no means implies that the twelvefold formula of PS should not be understood as defining the conditional structure of *saṃsāra* throughout successive lives. It must also be remembered that this discussion takes place with a non-Buddhist ascetic who has not yet gained confidence in the Buddha. It would thus not have been appropriate for the Buddha to reveal to him profound matters that could be penetrated only by one of mature wisdom.

Ven. Ñāṇavīra tries to buttress his non-temporal interpretation of PS with a brief quotation from the Mahātaṇhāsaṅkhaya Sutta. In that sutta, at the end of a long catechism that explores the twelvefold series of PS in both the order of origination and the order of cessation, the Buddha says to the monks:

> "I have presented you, monks, with this Dhamma that is visible (*sandiṭṭhika*), immediate (*akālika*), inviting one to come and see, accessible, to be personally realized by the wise."

Ven. Ñāṇavīra supposes that "this Dhamma" refers to *paṭicca-samuppāda*, and that the description of it as *akālika* must mean that the entire formula defines a non-temporal configuration of factors.

If we turn to the sutta from which the quotation comes, we would find that Ven. Ñāṇavīra's supposition is directly contradicted by the sequel to the statement on which he bases his thesis. In that sequel (M I 265–70), the Buddha proceeds to illustrate the abstract terms of the PS formula, first with an account of the life process of the blind worldling who is swept up in the forward cycle of origination, and then with an account of the noble disciple, who brings the cycle to a stop. Here temporal succession is in evidence throughout the exposition. The life process begins with conception in the womb (elsewhere expressed as "the descent of consciousness" into the womb and the "taking shape of name-and-form" in the womb—DN 15/D II 63). After the period of gestation comes birth, emergence from the mother's womb, followed in turn by: the gradual maturation of the sense faculties (= the six sense bases), exposure to the five cords of sensual pleasure (= contact), intoxication with pleasant feelings (= feeling), seeking delight in feelings (= craving). Then come clinging, becoming, birth, and aging and death. Here a sequence of two lives is explicitly defined, while the past life is implied by the *gandhabba*, cited as one of the conditions for conception of the embryo to occur. The *gandhabba* or "spirit," other texts indicate (see M II 157), is the stream of consciousness of a deceased person coming from the preceding life, and this factor is just as essential to conception as the sexual union of the parents, which it must utilize as its vehicle for entering the womb.

In the contrasting passage on the wise disciple, we see how an individual who has taken birth through the same past causes goes forth as a monk in the Buddha's dispensation, undertakes the training, and breaks the link between feeling and craving. Thereby he puts an end to the future renewal of the cycle of becoming. By extinguishing "delight in feelings," a manifestation of craving, he terminates clinging, becoming, birth, aging, and death, and thereby arrives at the cessation of the entire mass of suffering. Thus here, in the very sutta from which the description of PS as "timeless" is drawn, we see the sequence of PS factors illustrated in a way that indubitably involves temporal succession.

In order to determine what the word *akālika* means in relation to PS, we must carefully examine its contextual usage in the suttas on PS. Such suttas are rare, but in the Nidāna-saṃyutta we find one text that can help resolve this problem. In this sutta (SN 12:33/S II 56–59), the Buddha enumerates forty-four "cases of knowledge" (*ñāṇavatthu*) arranged into eleven tetrads. There is knowledge of each factor of PS from *jarāmaraṇa* back to *saṅkhārā*, each defined according to the standard definitions; then there is knowledge of its origination through its condition, of its cessation through the cessation of its condition, and of the Noble Eightfold Path as the way to cessation. With respect to each tetrad, the Buddha says (taking the first as an example):

> "When the noble disciple understands thus aging and death, its origin, its cessation, and the way leading to its cessation, this is his knowledge of the principle (or law: *dhamme ñāṇa*). By means of this principle which is seen, understood, *akālika*, attained, fathomed, he applies the method to the past and the future. When he does so, he knows: 'Whatever recluses and brahmins in the past understood aging and death (etc.), all understood them as I do now; whatever recluses and brahmins in the future will understand aging and death (etc.), all will understand them as I do now.' This is his knowledge of the consequence (*anvaye ñāṇa*)."

If we consider the word *akālika* as employed here, the meaning cannot be "non-temporal" in the sense either that the items conjoined by the conditioning relationship occur simultaneously or that they altogether transcend temporal differentiation. For the same sutta defines birth and death with the stock formulas—'birth' as birth into any of the orders of beings, etc., 'death' as the passing away from any of the orders of beings, etc. (see § 7 above). Surely these events, birth and death, cannot be either simultaneous or extra-temporal. But the word *akālika* is here set in correlation with a series of words signifying knowledge, and this gives us the key to its meaning. Taken in context, the word qualifies, not the factors such as birth and death themselves, but the principle (*dhamma*) that is seen and understood. The point made by calling the principle *akālika* is that this principle is known and seen immediately, that is, that the conditional relationship between any two terms is known directly with perceptual certainty. Such immediate knowledge is contrasted with knowledge of the consequence, or inferential knowledge (*anvaye ñāṇa*), by which the disciple does not grasp a principle by immediate insight but by reflection on what the principle entails.

Exactly the same conclusion regarding the meaning of *akālika* would follow if we return to the passage from M I 265 quoted above (§ 25) and examine it more closely in context. We would then see that the Buddha does not link the statement that the Dhamma is *sandiṭṭhiko akāliko* to the formulation of PS in any way that suggests the factors or their relationships are non-temporal. The statement does not even follow immediately upon the catechism on PS. Rather, after questioning the monks in detail about the PS formula, the Buddha asks them whether they would speak as they do (i.e. affirming the connections established by the formula) merely out of respect for him as their Teacher; the monks answer in the negative. He then asks, "Isn't it the case that you speak only of what you have known for yourselves, seen for yourselves, understood for yourselves?" To this the monks reply, "Yes, venerable sir." At this point the Buddha says: "I have presented you, monks, with this Dhamma that is visible, immediate...." Each of the terms in this stock formula conveys, from a slightly different angle, the same essential point: that the Dhamma is something that can be seen (*sandiṭṭhiko*); that it is to be known immediately (*akāliko*); that it calls out for personal verification (*ehipassiko*); that it is accessible (*opanayiko*); that it is to be personally realized by the wise (*paccattaṃ veditabbo viññūhi*). The terms all highlight, not the intrinsic nature of the Dhamma, but its relation to human knowledge and understanding. They are all epistemological in import, not ontological; they are concerned with how the Dhamma is to be known, not with the temporal status of the known.

Again, the conclusion is established: The Dhamma (inclusive of *paṭicca-samuppāda*) is *akālika* because it is to be known immediately by direct inspection, not by inference or by faith in the word of another. Thus, although birth and death may be separated by 70 or 80 years, one ascertains immediately that death occurs in dependence on birth and cannot occur if there is no birth. Similarly, although the ignorance and *saṅkhārā* that bring about the descent of consciousness into the womb are separated from consciousness by a gap of lifetimes, one ascertains immediately that the descent of consciousness into the womb has come about through ignorance and *saṅkhārā*. And again, although future becoming, birth, and aging and death are separated from present craving and clinging by a gap of lifetimes, one ascertains immediately that if craving and clinging persist until the end of the lifespan, they will bring about reconception, and hence engender a future cycle of becoming. It is in this sense that the Buddha declares *paṭicca-samuppāda* to be *sandiṭṭhika, akālika*—"directly visible, immediate"—not in the sense that the terms of the formula have nothing to do with time or temporal succession.

## 10. The Knowledge of Final Deliverance

I will conclude this critique by highlighting one particularly disquieting consequence entailed by Ven. Ñāṇavīra's assertion that *paṭicca-samuppāda* has nothing to do with rebirth, with temporal succession, or with *kamma* and its fruit. Now the Suttas indicate that the arahants know that they have terminated the succession of births; this is their knowledge and vision of final deliverance (*vimuttiñāṇadassana*). Everywhere in the texts we see that when they attain liberation, they exclaim: "Destroyed is birth, the holy life has been lived, what had to be done has been done, there is no more (coming back) to this world," or: "This is my last birth; now there is no more re-becoming." These statements, found throughout the Canon, indicate that the arahants know for themselves that they are liberated from the round of rebirths.

Investigation of the texts will also show that the ground for the arahant's assurance regarding his liberation is his knowledge of *paṭicca-samuppāda*, particularly in the sequence of cessation. By seeing in himself the destruction of the āsavas, the "cankers" of sensual craving, craving for becoming, and ignorance, the arahant knows that the entire series of factors mentioned in PS has come to an end: ignorance, craving, clinging, and kammically potent volitional activities have ended in this present life, and no more compound of the five aggregates, subject to birth and death, will arise in the future. Perhaps the clearest example of this is the Kaḷāra-sutta (SN 12:32/S II 51–53). When the Buddha asks Venerable Sāriputta how he can declare "Destroyed is birth," he replies in terms of the destruction of its cause, *bhava*, and the Buddha's questioning leads him back along the chain of conditions to *vedanā*, for which he no longer has any craving.

Since knowledge of *paṭicca-samuppāda* in its aspect of cessation is the basis for the arahant's knowledge that he has destroyed birth and faces no more re-becoming in the future, if this formula does not describe the conditional structure of *saṃsāra* it is difficult to see how the arahant could have definite knowledge that he has reached the end of *saṃsāra*. If arahants have to accept it on trust from the Buddha that *saṃsāra* exists and can be terminated (as Ven. Ñāṇavīra would hold of those arahants who lack direct knowledge of past births), then those arahants would also have to accept it on trust from the Buddha that they have attained release from *saṃsāra*. Such a denouement to the entire quest for the Deathless would be far from satisfactory indeed.

It seems that Ven. Ñāṇavīra, in his eagerness to guarantee an immediate solution to the present problem of existential anxiety, has arrived at that solution by closing off the door to a direct ascertainment that one has solved the existential problem that the Suttas regard as paramount, namely, the beginningless problem of our beginningless bondage to *saṃsāra*. Fortunately, however, the Suttas confirm that the noble disciple does have direct knowledge that all beings bound by ignorance and craving dwell within beginningless *saṃsāra*, and that the destruction of ignorance brings cessation of becoming, Nibbāna. Consider how Venerable Sāriputta explains the faculty of understanding (and I stress that this is the faculty of understanding (*paññindriya*), not the faculty of faith):

> "When, lord, a noble disciple has faith, is energetic, has set up mindfulness, and has a concentrated mind, it can be expected that he will understand thus: 'This *saṃsāra* is without discoverable beginning; no first point can be discerned of beings roaming and wandering on, obstructed by ignorance and fettered by craving. But with the remainderless fading away and ceasing of

ignorance, a mass of darkness, this is the peaceful state, this is the sublime state: the stilling of all formations, the relinquishing of all acquisitions, the destruction of craving, dispassion, cessation, Nibbāna.' That understanding, lord, is his faculty of understanding."

The Buddha not only applauds this statement with the words "Sādhu, sādhu!" but to certify its truth he repeats Ven. Sāriputta's words in full.

# Review of Buddhism without Beliefs

It has often been said that Western Buddhism is distinguished from its Asian prototype by three innovative shifts: the replacement of the monastery by the lay community as the principal arena of Buddhist practice; the enhanced position of women; and the emergence of a grass-roots engaged Buddhism aimed at social and political transformation. These three developments, however, have been encompassed by a fourth which is so much taken for granted that it is barely noticed. This last innovation might be briefly characterized as an attempt to transplant Buddhist practice from its native soil of faith and doctrine into a new setting governed by largely secular concerns. For Asian Buddhists, including Eastern masters teaching in the West, this shift is so incomprehensible as to be invisible, while Western Buddhists regard it as so obvious that they rarely comment on it.

Stephen Batchelor, however, has clearly discerned the significance of this development and what it portends for the future. Having been trained in Asia in two monastic lineages (Tibetan Gelugpa and Korean Soen) and relinquished his monk's vows to live as a lay Buddhist teacher in the West, he is acquainted with both traditional Buddhism and its Western offshoots. His book *Buddhism without Beliefs*[24] is an intelligent and eloquent attempt to articulate the premises of the emerging secular Buddhism and define the parameters of a "dharma[25] practice" appropriate to the new situation. Batchelor is a highly gifted writer with a special talent for translating abstract explanation into concrete imagery drawn from everyday life. His book is obviously the product of

24. *Buddhism without Beliefs: A Contemporary Guide to Awakening*; New York: Riverhead Books, 1997.

25. In accordance with his own convention, I have used "dharma" when quoting or closely paraphrasing Batchelor, and "Dhamma" when making general remarks and to express my own ideas.

serious reflection and a deep urge to make the Dhamma viable in our present sceptical age. Whether his vision is adequate to that aim is a tantalizing question that I hope to explore in this review.

The book is divided into three parts, each with several short sections. In the first part, entitled "Ground," Batchelor sketches the theoretical framework of his "Buddhism without beliefs." He begins by drawing a sharp distinction between two entities so closely intertwined in Buddhist history that they seem inseparable, but which, he holds, must be severed for the Dhamma to discover its contemporary relevance. One is "dharma practice," the Buddha's teaching as a path of training aimed at awakening and freedom from "anguish" (his rendering of *dukkha*); the other is "Buddhism," a system of beliefs and observances geared towards social stability and religious consolation. For Batchelor, the religious expressions and worldview in which the Dhamma has come down to us have no intrinsic connection to the core of the Buddha's teaching. They pertain solely to the Asian cultural soil within which Buddhism took root. While they may have served a purpose in earlier times, in relation to the continuing transmission of the Dhamma, they are more a hindrance than a help.

According to Batchelor, if the Dhamma is to offer an effective alternative to mainstream thought and values, it must be divested of its religious apparel and recast in a purely secular mode. What then emerges is an "agnostic" style of dharma practice aimed at personal and social liberation from the suffering created by egocentric clinging. On the great questions to which religious Buddhism provides answers—the questions concerning our place in the grand scheme of things—Batchelor's agnostic version of the Dhamma takes no stand. In his view "the dharma is not something to believe in but something to do" (p. 17).

At first glance, Batchelor's approach seems to echo the Buddha's advice in his famous simile about the man struck with the poisoned arrow (MN 63): "Just practice the path and don't speculate about metaphysical questions." However, are the two really pointing in the same direction? I don't think so. Batchelor seems curiously ambivalent about his purpose relative to the historical Buddha. He begins as if he intended to salvage the authentic vision of the Buddha from the cultural accretions that have obscured its pristine clarity; yet, when he runs up against principles taught by the Buddha that collide with his own agenda, he does not hesitate to discard them. This suggests more than cultural accretions are at stake.

From the Buddha's silence on the metaphysical questions of his day and his teaching's focus on suffering and its cessation, Batchelor concludes that the Buddha's teaching should be viewed as "an existential, therapeutic, and liberating agnosticism" (p. 15). A look at the Pāli suttas, however, will show us that while the Buddha did not answer the ten "undetermined questions," he made quite explicit pronouncements on questions that Batchelor would wave aside. In a telling passage, Batchelor states that an agnostic Buddhist would not turn to the dharma to answer questions about "where we came from, where we are going, what happens after death . . . [but] would seek such knowledge in the appropriate domains: astrophysics, evolutionary biology, neuroscience, etc."(p. 18). From Batchelor's point of view, this implies that in his metaphysical comments, the Buddha was stepping outside his own domain and trespassing on that of science—doubly ironic, since responsible scientists usually admit such questions are unanswerable or belong in the domain of religion rather than science.

Batchelor tries to escape this predicament by suggesting that, in speaking of rebirth, the Buddha was merely adopting "the symbols, metaphors, and imagery of his world" (p. 15). However, he later admits that the Buddha "accepted" the ideas of rebirth and kamma, yet he still finds it "odd that a practice concerned with anguish and the ending of anguish should be obliged to adopt ancient Indian metaphysical theories and thus accept as an article of faith that consciousness cannot be explained in terms of brain function" (p. 37). Batchelor cannot endorse these "metaphysical theories." While he does not reject the idea of rebirth, he claims that the most honest approach we can take to the whole issue of life after death is simply acknowledging that we don't know. Accepting the doctrines of rebirth and kamma, even on the authority of the Buddha, indicates a "failure to summon forth the courage to risk a nondogmatic and nonevasive stance on such crucial existential matters" (p. 38).

To justify his interpretation of the Dhamma, Batchelor uses arguments that gain their cogency through selective citation, oversimplification, and rationalization. For example, when discussing the "four ennobling truths," Batchelor points out (in accordance with the First Sermon) that these truths are "not propositions to believe

[but] challenges to act" (p. 7). This, however, is only partly true: in order to act upon truths, one has to believe them. More pointedly, Batchelor fails to acknowledge that the tasks imposed by the truths acquire their meaning from a specific context—the quest for liberation from the vicious cycle of rebirths (see MN 26; SN Chapter 15). Lifting the four Noble Truths out of their original context shared by the Buddha and his adherents and transposing them into a purely secular framework alters their meaning in crucial ways. We see this when Batchelor interprets the first truth as "existential anguish." For the Buddha and subsequent sacred tradition, dukkha really means the suffering of repeated becoming in the round of rebirths. Thus, if one dismisses the idea of rebirth, the Four Truths lose their depth and scope.

The sharp dichotomy that Batchelor posits between "dharma practice" and "religious Buddhism" also is hard to endorse. Rather, we should recognize a spectrum of Buddhist practices, ranging from simple devotional and ethical observances to more advanced contemplative and philosophical explorations. What makes them specifically part of the Buddhist Dhamma is that they are all enfolded in a distinctive matrix of faith and understanding that disappears when "dharma practice" is pursued based on different presuppositions. Batchelor describes the premises that underlie traditional lay Buddhist practice, such as kamma and rebirth, as mere "consolatory elements" that have crept in to the Dhamma and blunted its critical edge (pp. 18–19). Yet, to speak thus is to forget that such principles were repeatedly taught by the Buddha himself, and not always for the sake of consolation, as a glance through the Pāli Nikāyas would show.

Even the notion that Buddhist religiosity is defined by a set of now unquestioned beliefs seems to derive its plausibility from viewing Buddhism in terms of a Christian model. Dhamma practice as taught by the Buddha makes no demands for blind faith; the invitation to question and investigate is always extended. One first approaches the Dhamma by testing those teachings of the Buddha that come into the range of one's own experience. If they stand up under scrutiny, one then places faith in the teacher and accepts on trust those points of his teaching that one cannot personally validate. Collectively, all these principles make up Right View (*sammādiṭṭhi*), the first step of the Noble Eightfold Path. Subjecting the principles to insistent agnostic questioning, as Batchelor proposes, derails one's practice from the start. In the Buddha's version of the path, one begins with certain beliefs that serve as guidelines to Right Understanding and Right Practice. Then, when one's practice matures, initial belief is transcended by personal realization based on insight. Once one arrives at the far shore, one can leave behind the entire raft (see MN 22), but one doesn't discard the compass before one has even stepped on board.

The middle portion of the book is called "Path" and provides a sketch of Batchelor's agnostic conception of dharma practice. His explanations here are clear and lively, allowing him to display the creative side of his literary gifts. Notably absent in Batchelor's conception of the path is the traditional foundation for Buddhist practice: Going for Refuge to the Three Jewels. Of course, such an obviously religious act hardly makes sense in the framework of agnostic dharma practice. This omission, however, is quite significant, I think, because a world of difference must separate the practice of the agnostic dharma follower from that of the confirmed Buddhist who has gone for refuge. Batchelor mentions no code of moral rules, not even the Five Precepts. At several points, in fact, he speaks lightly of the codification of ethics, proposing moral integrity in its place. While his analysis of moral integrity includes some impressive insights, it remains questionable to me whether integrity alone, without concrete guidelines, is a sufficient basis for ethics.

In the final part, "Fruition," Batchelor explores the consequences of his conception of dharma practice as a "passionate agnosticism." He begins with an account of the meditative path that strikes me as very strange. As mindfulness develops, he explains, the process of meditation evolves into a radical, relentless questioning of every aspect of experience, until we find ourselves immersed in a profound perplexity that envelopes our whole being. For Batchelor, "this perplexed questioning is the central path itself" (p. 98), a path that does not seek any answers nor even a goal. For one like myself, nurtured on the Pāli texts, this seems a bizarre conception of "dharma practice." Granted, the purpose of meditation is not simply to gain confirmation of one's belief system, but does this justify using the raft of the Dhamma to founder in the treacherous sea of doubt, rather than to cross to the far shore? The Buddha repeatedly emphasized that insight meditation leads to direct knowledge of the true nature of things, a knowledge that pulls up doubt by its roots. This shows again the bearing of one's starting point on one's destination. If one starts off with the agnostic imperative, one descends ever deeper into mystery and doubt; if one places trust in the Dhamma and accedes to Right View, one's path culminates in Right Knowledge and Right Liberation (see MN 117).

In the last sections of the book, on "imagination" and "culture," Batchelor tackles the problem of the encounter between Buddhism and the contemporary world. He points out that throughout its history, the Dhamma has rejuvenated itself by continually altering its forms to respond to changing social and cultural conditions. This creative adjustment was an act of imagination, of creative vision, on the part of gifted Buddhist thinkers, who thereby gave birth to a fresh manifestation of the teaching. Later, however, institutionalized religious orthodoxy stepped in, placed the new forms under its authority, and thereby squelched the creative impulse imparted by the founders. Again, while I cannot deny that orthodoxy and creativity have had an uneasy relationship, I find Batchelor's version of Buddhist history too simplistic, almost as if he were viewing Buddhist orthodoxy merely as an imitation of institutionalized control and suppression seen in Western faiths. He also fails to acknowledge sufficiently the role of orthodoxy in encouraging Dhamma practice rather than suppressing it, which has facilitated the development of accomplished spiritual masters through the centuries. Orthodoxy and contemplative realization, though often at odds with each other, are not necessarily incompatible.

Batchelor argues that the meeting of Buddhism with the contemporary West requires creation, from the resources of the dharma, of a new "culture of awakening that addresses the specific anguish of the contemporary world" (p. 110). Such a culture must respond to the unprecedented situation we find today: the promise of spiritual liberation converging with universal striving for personal and social freedom. In attempting to create such a culture of awakening, he stresses the need for dharma followers to preserve the integrity of the Buddhist tradition while at the same time fulfilling their responsibility to the present and the future. With that much I am in full agreement, and I acknowledge that the problem is especially acute for Theravāda Buddhism, which historically has been tied to a very particular cultural environment. Nevertheless, I differ with Batchelor regarding what is central to the Dhamma and what is peripheral. In my view, Batchelor is ready to cast away too much that is integral to the Buddha's teaching in order to make it fit in with today's secular climate of thought. I'm afraid that the ultimate outcome of such concessions could be a psychologically oriented humanism tinged with Buddhist philosophy and a meditative mood. I certainly think that Buddhists should freely offer other religions and secular disciplines the full resources of their own tradition— philosophy, ethics, meditation and psychology—with perfect liberty to use them for their own ends: "The Tathāgata does not have a teacher's closed fist." But we still have to draw a sharp line between what the Buddha's Dhamma is and what is not: I would say all such practices undertaken outside the context of Going for Refuge are still on the hither side of the Dhamma, not yet within its fold.

When the secular presuppositions of modernity clash with the basic principles of Right Understanding stressed by the Buddha, I maintain there is no question which of the two must be abandoned. Saṃsāra as the beginningless round of rebirths, kamma as its regulative law, Nibbāna as a transcendent goal—surely these ideas will not get a rousing welcome from sceptical minds. A sense of refuge, renunciation and compassion based on the perception of universal suffering, a striving to break all mental bonds and fetters—surely these values are difficult in an age of easy pleasure. Yet, these are all so fundamental to the true Dhamma, so closely woven into its fabric, that to delete them is to risk nullifying its liberative power. If this means that Buddhism retains its character as a religion, so be it. I see nothing to fear in this; the greater danger comes from diluting the teaching so much that its potency is lost. The secularization of life and the widespread decline in moral values have had grave consequences throughout the world, jeopardizing our collective sanity and survival. Today a vast cloud of moral and spiritual confusion hangs over humankind, and Batchelor's agnostic dharma practice seems to me a very weak antidote indeed. In my view, what we require is a clear articulation of the essential principles taught by the Buddha himself in all their breadth and profundity. The challenge—and it is a difficult one—is to express these principles in a living language that addresses the deep crises of our time.

# The Jhānas and the Lay Disciple

## According to the Pāli Suttas

### 1. Introduction

The Pāli Nikāyas leave no doubt of the important role the jhānas play in the structure of the Buddhist path. In such texts as the Sāmaññaphala Sutta (DN 2), the Cūḷahatthipadopama Sutta (MN 27), and many others on the "gradual training" (*anupubbasikkhā*) of the Buddhist monk, the Buddha invariably introduces the jhānas to exemplify the training in concentration. When the bhikkhu has fulfilled the preliminary moral discipline, we read, he goes off into solitude and cleanses his mind of the "five hindrances." When his mind has been so cleansed, he enters and dwells in the four jhānas, described by a stock formula repeated countless times in the Nikāyas:

> Here, bhikkhus, secluded from sensual pleasures, secluded from unwholesome states, a bhikkhu enters and dwells in the first jhāna, which is accompanied by thought and examination, with rapture and happiness born of seclusion. With the subsiding of thought and examination, he enters and dwells in the second jhāna, which has internal confidence and unification of mind, is without thought and examination, and has rapture and happiness born of concentration. With the fading away as well of rapture, he dwells equanimous and, mindful and clearly comprehending, he experiences happiness with the body; he enters and dwells in the third jhāna of which the noble ones declare: "He is equanimous, mindful, one who dwells happily." With the abandoning of pleasure and pain, and with the previous passing away of joy and displeasure, he enters and dwells in the fourth jhāna, which is neither painful nor pleasant and includes the purification of mindfulness by equanimity.[26]

---

26. *Vivicc'eva kāmehi vivicca akusalehi dhammehi savitakkaṃ savicāraṃ vivekajaṃ pītisukhaṃ paṭhamaṃ jhānaṃ upasampajja viharati. Vitakka-*

In Theravada Buddhist circles during the past few decades a debate has repeatedly erupted over the question whether or not jhāna is necessary to attain the "paths and fruits," that is, the four graded stages of enlightenment. The debate has been sparked off by the rise to prominence of the various systems of insight meditation that have become popular both in Asia and the West, especially among lay Buddhists. Those who advocate such systems of meditation contend that the paths and fruits can be attained by developing insight (*vipassanā*) without a foundation of jhāna. This method is called the vehicle of bare insight (*suddha-vipassanā*), and those who practise in this mode are known as "dry insighters" (*sukkha-vipassaka*) because their practice of insight has not been "moistened" by prior attainment of the jhānas. Apparently, this system finds support from the *Visuddhimagga* and the Pāli Commentaries, though it is not given a very prominent place in the commentarial treatment of the path, which usually follows the canonical model in placing the jhānas before the development of insight.[27]

To help answer the question whether the jhānas are necessary for the attainment of the stages of awakening, we might narrow the question down by asking whether they are needed to reach the first stage of awakening, known as stream-entry (*sotāpatti*). Since the Nikāyas order the process of awakening into four stages—stream-entry, once-returning, non-returning, and arahantship—it is possible that the jhānas come to assume an essential role at a later stage in the unfolding of the path, and not at the first stages. Thus it may be that the insight required for the earlier stages does not presuppose prior attainment of the jhānas, while the jhānas become indispensable in making the transition from one of the intermediate stages to a more advanced stage. I myself believe there is strong evidence in

---

*vicārānaṃ vūpasamā ajjhattaṃ sampasādanaṃ cetaso ekodibhāvaṃ avitakkaṃ avicāraṃ samādhijaṃ pītisukhaṃ dutiyaṃ jhānaṃ upasam-pajja viharati. Pītiyā ca virāgā upekkhako ca viharati sato ca sampajāno sukhañca kāyena paṭisaṃvedeti, yan taṃ ariyā ācikkhanti upekkhako satimā sukhavihārī ti tatiyaṃ jhānaṃ upasampajja viharati. Sukhassa ca pahānā dukkhassa ca pahānā pubb'eva somanassadoman-assānaṃ atthagamā adukkham asukhaṃ upekkhāsatipārisuddhiṃ catutthaṃ jhānaṃ upasampajja viharati.*

27. The vehicle of bare insight is mentioned at Vism XVIII.5 (PTS ed. p. 558); the dry insighter at XXI.112 (p. 666) and XXIII.18 (p. 702). See too Spk commenting on SN 12:70/S II 119–128.

the Nikāyas that the jhānas become an essential factor for those intent on advancing from the stage of once-returning to that of non-returner. I will review the texts that corroborate this thesis later in this paper.

Recently, however, several articulate teachers of meditation have argued down the validity of the dry insight approach, insisting that the jhānas are necessary for the successful development of insight at every stage. Their arguments usually begin by making a distinction between the standpoints of the Pāli Canon and the Commentaries. On this basis, they maintain that from the perspective of the Canon jhāna is needed to attain even stream-entry. The Nikāyas themselves do not address this problem in clear and unambiguous terms, and it is difficult to derive from them any direct pronouncement on its resolution. In the suttas dealing with the gradual training, all the stages of awakening are telescoped into one series, and thus no differentiation is made between the preparatory attainments required for stream-entry, once-returning, non-returning, and arahantship. We simply see the monk go off into solitude, attain the four jhānas, and then proceed directly to arahantship, called "the knowledge of the destruction of the taints." From such texts, there can be no denying the role of the jhānas in bringing the path to fulfillment, but here I shall be concerned principally with the question whether or not they are categorically necessary to win the first fruit of the path.

In pursuing this question I intend to pick up an important but generally neglected clue the suttas lay at our doorstep. This is the fact that many of the Buddha's followers who attained the first three stages of awakening, from stream-entry through non-returning, were lay people. The only stage that the Canon depicts as the near-exclusive domain of monks and nuns is arahantship.[28] This clue is more important than might appear at first glance, for a close

---

28. For example, at D II 92 the Buddha testifies that numerous lay disciples who had died had reached the first three stages, and at M I 490–91 he declares that he has "many more than five hundred" lay disciples who have become non-returners. The question of lay arahantship is a vexed one. While the texts record several cases of lay people who attained arahantship, immediately afterwards they either take ordination or expire. This is the basis for the traditional belief that if a lay person attains arahantship, he or she either enters the Sangha that very day or passes away.

examination of texts describing the personal qualities and lifestyles of noble lay disciples might bring to light just the material we need to unravel the knots tied into this perplexing issue.

A study of the Nikāyas as a whole would show that they depict classes of disciples in terms of paradigms or archetypes. These paradigms are generally constructed with extreme rigor and consistency, indicating that they are evidently governed by a precisely determined scheme. Yet, somewhat strangely, it is rare for the outlines of this scheme to be spelled out in the abstract. This puts the burden on us to elicit from the relevant suttas the underlying principles that govern the portrayal of types. The texts with which we are concerned delineate disciples at different levels of development by way of clusters of specific qualities and practices. These texts function both descriptively and prescriptively. They show us what kinds of qualities we can normally expect of disciples at particular stages of progress, and thereby they imply (and sometimes state) what kinds of practices an aspirant at a lower stage should take up to advance further along the path.

To draw upon suttas dealing with lay disciples is to approach the question of the need for jhāna from an angle somewhat different from the one usually adopted. Most participants in this discussion have focused on texts dealing principally with monastic practice. The drawback to this approach, as indicated above, lies in the predilection of the Nikāyas to compress the successive levels of monastic attainment into a single comprehensive scheme without showing how the various levels of practice are to be correlated with the successive stages of attainment.[29] So instead of working with these monastic texts, I intend to turn my spotlight on the unordained segment of the Buddhist community and look at suttas that discuss the spiritual practices and qualities of the lay noble disciple. For if the jhānas are truly necessary to attain stream-entry, then they should be just as much integral to the practice of the lay follower as they are to the practice of the monk, and thus we should find texts that regularly ascribe jhānic practice and attainment to lay disciples just as we find them in the case of monks. If, on the other hand, the texts consistently describe the practices and qualities of certain types

29. One such text which does make the correlations, in a monastic context, is AN 3:85/A I 231–32, which I will discuss below.

of noble lay disciples in ways that pass over or exclude the jhānas, then we have strong grounds for concluding that the jhānas are not prerequisites for attaining discipleship at these levels.

I will frame my study around three specific questions:

(1) Do the texts indicate that a worldling must attain jhāna before entering upon the "fixed course of rightness" (*sammatta-niyāma*), the irreversible path to stream-entry?
(2) Do the texts typically ascribe the jhānas to lay disciples who have attained stream-entry?
(3) If the texts do not normally attribute the jhānas to the stream-enterer, is there any stage in the maturation of the path where their attainment becomes essential?

## 2. Jhāna and the Attainment of Stream-entry

Let us turn directly to the texts themselves to see if they can shed any light on our problem. When we do survey the Nikāyas with this issue in mind we find, perhaps with some astonishment, that they neither lay down a clear stipulation that jhāna is needed to attain stream-entry nor openly assert that jhāna is dispensable. The Sutta Piṭaka mentions four preconditions for reaching the path, called *sotāpattiyaṅga*, factors of stream-entry, namely: association with superior people (i.e., with the noble ones); listening to the true Dhamma; proper attention; and practice in accordance with the Dhamma.[30] It would seem that all the elements of Buddhist meditative practice, including the jhānas, should come under the fourth factor, but the Nikāyas themselves do not state whether "practice in accordance with the Dhamma" includes the jhānas. The few texts that specify what is actually meant by "practice in accordance with the Dhamma" are invariably concerned with insight meditation. They employ a fixed formula, with variable subjects, to describe a bhikkhu practising in such a way. Two suttas define such practice as aimed at the cessation of the factors of dependent origination (SN 12:16/S II 18, SN 12:67/S II 115); another, as aimed at the cessation of the five aggregates (SN 22:115/S III 163–64); and still another, as aimed at the cessation of the

30. *Sappurisasaṃseva, saddhammasavana, yoniso manasikāra, dhammānudhammapaṭipadā*. See SN 55:55/S V 410–11.

six sense bases (SN 35:155/S IV 141). Of course, meditation practice undertaken to attain the jhānas would have to be included in "practice in accordance with the Dhamma," but the texts give no ground for inferring that such practice is a prerequisite for reaching stream-entry.

A stream-enterer is endowed with four other qualities, mentioned often in the Sotāpatti-saṃyutta (SN chap. 55). These, too, are called *sotāpattiyaṅga*, but in a different sense than the former set. These are the factors that qualify a person as a stream-enterer. The first three are "confirmed confidence" (*aveccappasāda*) in the Buddha, the Dhamma, and the Saṅgha; the fourth is "the virtues dear to the noble ones," generally understood to mean inviolable adherence to the Five Precepts. From this, we can reasonably suppose that in the preliminary stage leading up to stream-entry the aspirant will need firm faith in the Three Jewels (the Buddha, the Dhamma, and the Saṅgha) and scrupulous observance of the Five Precepts. Further, the realization of stream-entry itself is often depicted as a cognitive experience of almost ocular immediacy. It is called the gaining of the eye of the Dhamma (*dhammacakkhu-paṭilābha*), the breakthrough to the Dhamma (*dhammābhisamaya*), the penetration of the Dhamma (*dhamma-paṭivedha*).[31] One who has undergone this experience is said to have "seen the Dhamma, reached the Dhamma, understood the Dhamma, fathomed the Dhamma."[32] Taken together, both modes of description—by way of the four factors of stream-entry and by way of the event of realization—indicate that the disciple has arrived at stream-entry primarily through insight supported by unwavering faith in the Three Jewels. It is noteworthy that the texts on the realization of stream-entry make no mention of any prior accomplishment in jhāna as a prerequisite for reaching the path. In fact, several texts show the breakthrough to stream-entry as occurring to someone without any prior meditative experience, simply by listening to the Buddha or an enlightened monk give a discourse on the Dhamma.[33]

31. *Dhammacakkhu-paṭilābha, dhammābhisamaya, dhamma-paṭivedha*. See S II 134–38 for the first two; the third is more a commentarial expression used to explain the second.

32. *Diṭṭhadhamma, pattadhamma, viditadhamma, pariyogāḷhadhamma*; at e.g. D I 110, M I 501, etc.

33. D I 110, M I 501, as well as S III 106, 135, etc.

While the process of "entering the stream" involves both faith and wisdom, individuals differ in their disposition with respect to these two qualities: some are disposed to faith, others to wisdom. This difference is reflected in the division of potential stream-enterers into two types, known as the *saddhānusārī* or faith-follower and the *dhammānusārī* or Dhamma-follower. Both have entered "the fixed course of rightness" (*sammatta-niyāma*), the irreversible path to stream-entry, by attuning their understanding of actuality to the nature of actuality itself, and thus for both insight is the key to entering upon the path. The two types differ, however, in the means by which they generate insight. The faith-follower, as the term implies, does so with faith as the driving force; inspired by faith, he resolves on the ultimate truth and thereby gains the path. The Dhamma-follower is driven by an urge to fathom the true nature of actuality; inspired by this urge, he investigates the teaching and gains the path. When they have known and seen the truth of the Dhamma, they realize the fruit of stream-entry.

Perhaps the most informative source on the difference between these two types is the Okkantika-saṃyutta, where the Buddha shows how they enter upon the fixed course of rightness:

> "Bhikkhus, the eye is impermanent, changing, becoming otherwise. So too the ear ... nose ... tongue ... body ... mind. One who places faith in these teachings and resolves on them thus is called a faith-follower: he is one who has entered the fixed course of rightness, entered the plane of the superior persons, transcended the plane of the worldlings. He is incapable of doing any deed by reason of which he might be reborn in hell, in the animal realm, or in the sphere of ghosts; he is incapable of passing away without having realized the fruit of stream-entry.
>
> "One for whom these teachings are accepted thus to a sufficient degree by being pondered with wisdom is called a Dhamma-follower: he is one who has entered the fixed course of rightness ... (he is) incapable of passing away without having realized the fruit of stream-entry.

> "One who knows and sees these teachings thus is called a stream-enterer, no longer bound to the nether world, fixed in destiny, with enlightenment as his destination."[34]

It is noteworthy that this passage makes no mention of jhāna. While prior experience of jhāna would no doubt help to make the mind a more fit instrument for insight, it is surely significant that jhāna is not mentioned either as an accompaniment of the "entry upon the fixed course of rightness" or as a prerequisite for it.

It might be objected that several other passages on the two candidates for stream-entry implicitly include the jhānas among their meditative equipment. The details of these passages need not concern us here. What is of interest to us is that they assign to both the faith-follower and the Dhamma-follower the five spiritual faculties: faith, energy, mindfulness, concentration, and wisdom.[35] The Indriya-saṃyutta states that the faculty of concentration "is to be seen among the four jhānas,"[36] and a definition of the concentration faculty includes the formula for the jhānas.[37] Thus, if we argue deductively from these ascriptions and definitions, it would seem to follow as a matter of logic that both the Dhamma-

34. SN 25:1/S III 224: *Cakkhuṃ bhikkhave aniccaṃ vipariṇāmiṃ aññathābhāvi. Sotam ... mano anicco vipariṇāmī aññathābhāvī. Yo bhikkhave ime dhamme evaṃ saddahati adhimuccati, ayaṃ vuccati saddhānusārī okkanto sammattaniyāmaṃ sappurisabhūmiṃ okkanto vītivatto puthujjanabhūmiṃ. Abhabbo taṃ kammaṃ kātuṃ yaṃ kammaṃ katvā nirayaṃ vā tiracchānayoniṃ vā pettivisayaṃ vā upapajjeyya. Abhabbo ca tāva kālaṃ kātuṃ yāva na sotāpattiphalaṃ sacchikaroti. Yassa kho bhikkhave ime dhammā evaṃ paññāya mattaso nijjhānaṃ khamanti, ayaṃ vuccati dhammānusārī okkanto sammattaniyāmaṃ ... Abhabbo ca tāva kālaṃ kātuṃ yāva na sotāpattiphalaṃ sacchikaroti. Yo bhikkhave ime dhamme evaṃ jānāti evaṃ passati, ayaṃ vuccati sotāpanno avinipātadhammo niyato sambodhiparāyano.*

35. E.g., M I 479, S V 200–2. SN 55:25/S V 379 ascribes the five faculties to two types of persons who, though the terms are not used, are clearly identifiable as the *dhammānusārī* and *saddhānusārī.*

36. SN 48:8/S V 196: *catusu jhānesu, ettha samādhindriyaṃ daṭṭhabbaṃ.* See too AN 5:15/III 12, where it is said that the power of concentration (*samādhibala*) "is to be seen among the four jhānas."

37. At SN 48:10/S V 198, the faculty of concentration is defined by the formula for the four jhānas. At AN 5:14/A III 11, the power of concentation (*samādhibala*) is similarly defined.

follower and the faith-follower possess the jhānas. More broadly, since these faculties and powers belong to all noble disciples, not to monks alone, this might be held up as proof that all noble disciples, monks and lay followers, invariably possess the jhānas.

Such a conclusion would follow if we adopt a literal and deductive approach to the interpretation of the texts, but it is questionable whether such a hermeneutic is always appropriate when dealing with the formulaic definitions employed so often by the Nikāyas. To extract the intended meaning from such schematic definition, we require greater sensitivity to context, sensitivity guided by acquaintance with a wide assortment of relevant texts. Further, if we do opt for the literalist approach, then, since the passage simply inserts the formula for the four jhānas without qualification into the definition of the concentration faculty, we would have to conclude that all noble disciples, monks and lay followers alike, possess all four jhānas, not just one. Even more, they would have to possess the four jhānas already as faith-followers and Dhamma-followers, at the very entry to the path. This, however, seems too generous, and indicates that we need to be cautious in interpreting such formulaic definitions. In the case presently being considered, I would regard the use of the jhāna formula here as a way of showing the most eminent type of concentration to be developed by the noble disciple. I would not take it as a rigid pronouncement that all noble disciples actually possess all four jhānas, or even one of them.

But there is more to be said. When we attend closely to these texts, we see that a degree of flexibility is already built into them. In the analysis of the faculties at SN 48:9–10/S V 197–98, the first sutta offers an alternative definition of the faculty of concentration that does not mention the four jhānas, while the following sutta gives both definitions conjointly. The alternative version runs thus: "And what, monks, is the faculty of concentration? Here, monks, a noble disciple gains concentration, gains one-pointedness of mind, having made release the object. This is called the faculty of concentration."[38]

The Nikāyas themselves nowhere explain exactly what is meant by the concentration gained by "having made release the

38. *Katamañca bhikkhave samādhindriyaṃ? Idha bhikkhave ariyasāvako vossaggārammaṇaṃ karitvā labhati samādhiṃ labhati cittassa ekaggataṃ. Idaṃ bhikkhave samādhindriyaṃ.*

object" (*vossaggārammaṇaṃ karitvā*), but they do elsewhere suggest that release (*vossagga*) is a term for Nibbāna.[39] The Commentary interprets this passage with the aid of the distinction between mundane (*lokiya*) and supramundane (*lokuttara*) concentration: the former consists in the form-sphere jhānas (and the access to these jhānas), the latter in the supramundane jhānas concomitant with the supramundane path.[40] On the basis of this distinction, the Commentary explains "the concentration that makes release the object" as the supramundane concentration of the noble path arisen with Nibbāna as object.[41] Thus if we feel obliged to interpret the faculty and power of concentration in the light of the jhāna formula, we might go along with the Commentary in regarding it as the supramundane jhāna pertaining to the supramundane path and fruit.

However, we need not agree with the Commentaries in taking the expression "having made release the object" so literally. We might instead interpret this phrase more loosely as characterizing a concentration aimed at release, that is, directed towards Nibbāna.[42] Then we can understand its referent as the concentration that functions as the basis for insight, both initially in the preparatory

---

39. Throughout the Magga-saṃyutta, the expression *vossagga-pariṇāmi*, "maturing in release," is used to describe the factors of the Noble Eightfold Path. This suggests that *vossagga*, as the goal of the path, is Nibbāna.

40. Below I will elaborate on the distinction between the form-sphere and supramundane jhānas.

41. Spk III 234, commenting on SN 48:9.

42. Paṭis III 586–87 seems to take this tack in commenting on the expression thus: "Having as object release: here release is Nibbāna, for Nibbāna is called release because it is the releasing of the conditioned, its relinquishment. Insight and the phenomena associated with it have Nibbāna as object, Nibbāna as support, because they are established on Nibbāna as their support in the sense of slanting towards it by way of inclination. Concentration is nondistraction distinguished into access and absorption (*upacārappanābhedo avikkhepo*), consisting in the one-pointedness of mind aroused by being established on Nibbāna, with that as cause by taking as object release of the phenomena produced therein. Concentration partaking of penetration (*nibbedhabhāgiyo samādhi*), aroused subsequent to insight, is described." From this, it seems that "concentration having release as its object" can be understood as a concentration aroused through the practice of insight meditation, aiming at the attainment of Nibbāna.

phase of practice and later in immediate conjunction with insight. This would allow us to ascribe to the noble disciple a degree of concentration strong enough to qualify as a faculty without compelling us to hold that he must possess jhāna. Perhaps the combined definition of the concentration faculty in SN 48:10 is intended to show that two courses are open to disciples. One is the route emphasizing strong concentration, along which one develops the jhānas as the faculty of concentration; the other is the route emphasizing insight, along which one develops concentration only to the degree needed for insight to arise. This concentration, though falling short of jhāna, could still be described as "concentration that makes release its object."

The faith-follower and the Dhamma-follower are the lowest members of a sevenfold typology of noble persons mentioned in the Nikāyas as an alternative to the more common scheme of "the four pairs of persons," the four path-attainers and the realizers of their respective fruits.[43] The seven fall into three groups. At the apex are the arahants, who are distinguished into two types: (i) "both-ways-liberated" arahants (*ubhatobhāgavimutta*), who gain release from the taints together with deep experience of the formless attainments; and (ii) "wisdom-liberated" arahants (*paññāvimutta*), who win release from the taints without such experience of the formless attainments. Next are three types in the intermediate range, from stream-enterers up to those on the path to arahantship. These are: (iii) the body-witness (*kāyasakkhī*), who has partly eliminated the taints and experiences the formless attainments; (iv) the view-attainer (*diṭṭhippatta*), who does not experience the formless attainments and has partly eliminated the taints, with emphasis on wisdom; and (v) the faith-liberated (*saddhāvimutta*), who does not experience the formless attainments and has partly eliminated the taints, with emphasis on faith. Any disciple at the six intermediate stages—from stream-enterer to one on the path to arahantship—can fall into any of these three categories; the distinctions among them are not determined by degree of progress but by mode of progress, whether through strong concentration, wisdom, or faith. Finally come the two kinds of *anusārī* (vi–vii), who are on the path to stream-entry.

---

43. The fullest discussion of this sevenfold typology is at M I 477–79. The seven types are also defined, somewhat differently, at Pp 14–15.

What is noteworthy about this list is that *samādhi*, as a faculty, does not determine a class of its own until after the fruit of stream-entry has been realized. That is, facility in concentration determines a distinct type of disciple among the arahants (as the both-ways-liberated arahant) and among the aspirants for the higher stages (as the body-witness), but not among the aspirants for stream-entry. In this lowest category we have only the faith-follower and the Dhamma-follower, who owe their status to faith and wisdom, respectively, but there is no type corresponding to the body-witness.[44]

From the omission of a class of disciples training for stream-entry who also enjoy the experience of the formless meditations, one might suppose that disciples below the level of stream-entry cannot gain access to the formless attainments. This supposition is not tenable, however, for the texts show that many of the ascetics and contemplatives in the Buddha's day (including his two teachers before his enlightenment) were familiar with the jhānas and formless attainments. Since these attainments are not dependent on the insight made uniquely available through the Buddha's teaching, the omission of such a class of jhāna-attainers among those on the way to stream-entry must be explained in some other way than by the supposition that such a class does not exist.

---

44. One possible exception to this statement is a curious sutta, AN 7:53/A IV 78. Here the Buddha begins by discussing the first six types, of which the first two are said to be "without residue" (*anupādisesa*), i.e., of defilements, which means that they are arahants; the next four are said to be "with residue" (*sa-upādisesa*), meaning they have some defilements and thus are not yet arahants. But in the seventh position, where we would expect to find the *saddhānusārī*, he inserts instead "the seventh type, the person who dwells in the signless" (*sattamaṃ animittavihāriṃ puggalaṃ*). This is explained as "a monk who, through non-attention to all signs, enters and dwells in the signless mental concentration" (*bhikkhu sabbanimittānaṃ amanasikārā animittaṃ cetosamādhiṃ upasampajja viharati*). This assertion seems to open up, as an alternative to the faith-follower, a class of aspirants for stream-entry who specialize in concentration. But this passage is unique in the Nikāyas and has not formed the basis for an alternative system of classification. Moreover, the commentary explains the "signless mental concentration" to be "strong insight concentration" (*balava-vipassanā-samādhi*), so called because it removes the signs of permanence, pleasure, and selfhood. (See Mp IV 40) Thus it is questionable whether even the recognition of this type means that *samatha* concentration determines a class of disciple on the path to stream-entry.

I would propose that while disciples prior to stream-entry may or may not possess the formless attainments, skill in this area does not determine a distinct type because powerful concentration is not a governing factor in the attainment of stream-entry. The way to stream-entry certainly requires a degree of concentration sufficient for the "eye of the Dhamma" to arise, but the actual movement from the stage of a worldling to that of a path-attainer is driven by either strong conviction or a probing spirit of inquiry, which respectively determine whether the aspirant is to become a faith-follower or a Dhamma-follower. Once, however, the path has been gained, then one's degree of accomplishment in concentration determines one's future mode of progress. If one gains the formless attainments one takes the route of the body-witness, culminating in release as a both-ways-liberated arahant. If one does not attain them, one takes the route of the view-attainer or faith-liberated trainee, culminating in release as a wisdom-liberated arahant. Since these distinctions relate only to the formless attainments and make no mention of the jhānas, it is reasonable to suppose that types (ii), (iv–v), and (vi–vii) may have possession of the form-sphere jhānas. But by making faith and wisdom the key factors in gaining the initial access to the path, this scheme leaves open the possibility that some stream-enterers, and perhaps those at still higher levels, may not have gained these jhānas at all.

## 3. JHĀNA AND RIGHT CONCENTRATION

Though the above discussion seems to imply that the path of stream-entry might be reached without prior attainment of jhāna, the thesis that jhāna is necessary at every stage of enlightenment claims powerful support from the canonical account of the Noble Eightfold Path, which defines the path factor of right concentration (*sammā samādhi*) with the stock formula for the four jhānas.[45] From this definition it might be argued that since right concentration is integral to the path, and since the jhānas form the content of right concentration, the jhānas are indispensable from the first stage of awakening to the last.

45. For example, at D II 313 and S V 10.

This conclusion, however, does not necessarily follow. Even if we agree that the definition of right concentration by way of the jhānas categorically means that the jhānas must be reached in the course of developing the path, this need not be taken to stipulate that they must be attained prior to attaining stream-entry. It could be that attainment of jhāna is necessary to complete the development of the path, becoming mandatory at a relatively late point in the disciple's progress. That is, it may be a prerequisite for reaching one of the higher paths and fruits, but may not be indispensable for reaching the first path and fruit. The Theravāda exegetical system found in the Pāli Commentaries handles this issue in a different way. Based on the Abhidhamma's classification of states of consciousness, the Commentaries distinguish two kinds of path: the preliminary (*pubbabhāga*) or mundane (*lokiya*) path and the supramundane (*lokuttara*) path.[46] Two kinds of jhānas, mundane and supramundane, correspond to these two kinds of path. The mundane jhānas are exalted states of consciousness (*mahaggata-citta*) developed in the preliminary path, as a preparation for reaching the supramundane path; technically, they are "form-sphere" states of consciousness (*rūpāvacara-citta*), that is, types of consciousness typical of the "form realm" and tending to rebirth in the form realm. The supramundane jhānas are supramundane states of consciousness (*lokuttara-citta*) identical with the supramundane paths or fruits themselves.

This distinction allows the Commentaries to hold simultaneously two theses regarding the relation of jhāna to the path: (i) every path and fruition attainment, from the stage of stream-entry up, is also a jhāna, and thus all path-attainers are attainers of supramundane jhāna; (ii) not all path-attainers have reached jhāna in the preliminary path leading up to the supramundane path, and thus they need not be attainers of mundane (or form-sphere) jhāna. These two theses can be reconciled because the paths and fruits always occur at a level of concentration corresponding to one of the four jhānas and thus may be considered jhānas in their own right, though jhānas

46. The distinction is found already in Dhs, in its analysis of the classes of wholesome consciousness pertaining to the sphere of form and the supramundane types of wholesome consciousness. See too the Jhāna-vibhaṅga (Abhidhamma-bhājanīya) of Vibh.

of the supramundane rather than mundane type. These jhānas are quite distinct from the mundane jhānas, the exalted states of concentration pertaining to the form-sphere (*rūpāvacara*). As all path-attainers necessarily attain supramundane jhāna, they fulfill the definition of right concentration in the Noble Eightfold Path, but they may not have attained the form-sphere jhānas prior to reaching the path. Those who do not attain jhāna develop a lower degree of concentration (called access concentration, *upacāra-samādhi*) which they use as a basis to arouse insight and thereby reach the supramundane path. When those meditators who arouse insight without prior attainment of jhāna reach the supramundane path, their path attainment occurs at the level of the first supramundane jhāna. Those who have already cultivated the mundane jhānas prior to attaining the path, it is said, generally attain a path that occurs at a jhānic level corresponding to their degree of achievement in the practice of the mundane jhānas.[47]

Though the Nikāyas do not clearly distinguish the two types of paths and jhānas, several suttas foreshadow this distinction, the most prominent among them being the Mahācattārīsaka Sutta.[48] The distinction becomes explicit in the Abhidhamma, where it is used as a basis for the definitions of the form-sphere and supramundane wholesome states of consciousness. The Commentaries go one step further and adopt this distinction as foundational to their entire method of exegesis. Although one is certainly not justified in reading the interpretative concepts of the Commentaries into the canonical

47. See Vism XXI.112–16.

48. MN 117. In this sutta the Buddha distinguishes five of the path factors, from right view through right livelihood, into two kinds, one "connected with taints, partaking of merit, ripening in the aggregates" (*sāsava puññabhāgiya upadhivepakka*), the other "noble, taintless, supramundane, a factor of the path" (*ariya anāsava lokuttara maggaṅga*). "Noble right concentration with its supports and requisites" (*ariya sammā samādhi sa-upanisa sa-parikkhāra*) is mental one-pointedness equipped with the other seven factors in their noble, supramundane dimension. If the latter is understood to be supramundane jhāna, then we might suppose the jhānas usually described in the training of the disciple are "connected with taints, partaking of merit, ripening in the aggregates." The texts never describe the jhānas in quite these terms, but some suttas imply their attainment leads only to a higher rebirth without necessarily conducing to deliverance. See note 63 below.

texts themselves, since the Commentaries feel obliged to explain the definition of right concentration as the four jhānas in a way that does not imply all path-attainers possess the form-sphere jhānas, this makes it plain that they did not regard the form-sphere jhānas as a prerequisite for attaining the path of stream-entry.

## 4. THE STREAM-ENTERER AND JHĀNA

The contention between the two parties in the contemporary debate might be recapitulated thus: Those who assert that jhāna is necessary for the attainment of stream-entry usually insist that a mundane (or form-sphere) jhāna must be secured before one can enter the supramundane path. Those who defend the dry-insight approach hold that a mundane jhāna is not indispensable, that a lower degree of concentration suffices as a basis for the cultivation of insight and the attainment of the path. Both parties usually agree that jhāna is part of the actual path experience itself. The issue that divides them is whether the concentration in the preliminary portion of the path must include a jhāna.

To decide this question, I wish to query the texts themselves and ask whether they show us instances of stream-enterers who are not attainers of the jhānas. Now while there are no suttas which flatly state that it is possible to become a stream-enterer without having attained at least the first jhāna, I think there are several that imply as much.

(1) Let us start with the Cūḷadukkhakkhandha Sutta (MN No. 14). The sutta opens when the Sakyan lay disciple Mahānāma, identified by the commentary as a once-returner, comes to the Buddha and presents him with a personal problem. Although he has long understood, through the guidance of the teaching, that greed, hatred, and delusion are corruptions of the mind (*cittassa upakkilesa*), such states still arise in him and overpower his mind. This troubles him and makes him wonder what the underlying cause might be. In his reply (M I 91) the Buddha says: "Even though a noble disciple has clearly seen with perfect wisdom that sensual pleasures give little satisfaction and are fraught with suffering and misery, rife with greater danger, if he does not achieve a rapture and happiness apart from sensual pleasures, apart from unwholesome states, or something more peaceful than this, then he is not beyond

being enticed by sensual pleasures." The first part of this statement implies that the subject is at least a stream-enterer, for he is referred to as a "noble disciple" (*ariya-sāvaka*). Though the term *ariya-sāvaka* is occasionally used in a loose sense that need not be taken to imply attainment of stream-entry, here the expression "seeing with perfect wisdom" seems to establish his identity as at least a stream-enterer. Yet the second part of the statement implies he does not possess even the first jhāna, for the phrase used to describe what he lacks ("a rapture and happiness apart from sensual pleasures, apart from unwholesome states") precisely echoes the wording of the basic formula for the first jhāna. The state "more peaceful than that" would, of course, be the higher jhānas.

(2) At AN 5:179/A III 211, the Buddha speaks, with reference to "a lay follower clothed in white" (*gihī odātavasana*), of four "pleasant dwellings in this very life pertaining to the higher mind" (*cattāro ābhicetasikā diṭṭhadhamma-sukhavihārā*). Now in relation to monks, the Nikāyas invariably use this expression to mean the four jhānas.[49] If it were considered commonplace, or even paradigmatic, for a lay noble disciple to attain the four jhānas, one would expect the Buddha to explain the above expression in the same way as he does for monks. But he does not. Rather, when he specifies what these "pleasant abidings" mean for the noble lay follower, he identifies them with the possession of the four "factors of stream-entry" (*sotāpattiyaṅga*), namely, confirmed confidence in the Buddha, the Dhamma, and the Saṅgha, and possession of "the virtues dear to the noble ones." This difference in explanation has important ramifications and is indicative of major differences in expectations regarding lay followers and monks.

(3) At AN VI 10/A III 284–88, the Sakyan noble Mahānāma again approaches the Buddha and inquires about the meditative practice of "a noble disciple who has reached the fruit and understood the message" (*ariyasāvako āgataphalo viññātasāsano*). Here again, it is clear from the epithets used that the question concerns a lay follower who has realized stream-entry or some higher stage. Further, at the end of each expository section, the Buddha stresses the ariyan stature of the disciple with the words: "This is called, Mahānāma, a noble disciple who among unrighteous humanity has

49. See, e.g., M I 356; AN 10:8/A V 11, etc.

attained righteousness, who among an afflicted humanity dwells unafflicted, who has entered the stream of the Dhamma and develops recollection of the Buddha" (and so for each object of recollection).[50]

In his reply the Buddha shows how the lay disciple takes up one of the six objects of recollection (*cha anussati*): the Three Jewels, morality, generosity, and the devas. As the disciple recollects each theme, his mind is not obsessed by lust, hatred, or delusion, but becomes upright (*ujugata*): "With an upright mind he gains the inspiration of the goal, the inspiration of the Dhamma, gladness connected with the Dhamma. When he is gladdened rapture arises, his body becomes tranquil, and he experiences happiness. For one who is happy the mind becomes concentrated."[51] As this passage shows, contemplation based on the Buddha (and the other objects of recollection) culminates in samādhi, yet the nature of this samādhi is not elucidated by way of the jhāna formula. In fact, the Nikāyas never ascribe to these reflective contemplations the capacity to induce jhāna, and this is expressly denied in the Commentaries, which hold that because these meditation subjects involve intensive use of discursive thought they can lead only as far as access concentration (*upacāra-samādhi*).

It thus seems that the type of concentration typically available to a lay noble disciple at the stage of stream-entry or once-returning is access concentration. This, of course, does not mean that stream-enterers and once-returners don't attain the jhānas, but only that the standard doctrinal structure does not ascribe the jhānas to them as essential equipment.

(4) Nor does the above sutta imply that a lay stream-enterer must remain content merely with excursions into access concentration and cannot develop the higher wisdom of insight. To the contrary, the Buddha includes the higher wisdom among the five excellent qualities he regularly ascribes to noble lay disciples: faith, virtue,

---

50. A III 285, etc.: *Ayaṃ vuccati Mahānāma ariyasāvako visamagatāya pajāya samappatto viharati, savyāpajjhāya pajāya avyāpajjho viharati, dhammasotaṃ samāpanno buddhānussatiṃ bhāveti.*

51. Ibid: *Ujugatacitto kho pana Mahānāma ariyasāvako labhati atthavedaṃ labhati dhammavedaṃ labhati dhammūpasaṃhitaṃ pāmujjaṃ; pamuditassa pīti jāyati, pītimanassa kāyo passambhati; passaddhakāyo sukhaṃ vediyati; sukhino cittaṃ samādhiyati.*

learning, generosity, and wisdom.[52] In several suttas of the Sotāpatti-saṃyutta, generosity and wisdom even replace virtue as the fourth factor of stream-entry, faith being included by "confirmed confidence" in the Three Jewels.[53] We should note that we do not find among these qualities any mention of samādhi or a formula for the jhānas. Yet we see that wisdom is defined in exactly the same terms used to define the wisdom of a monk in training (*sekha*). It is "the noble wisdom that discerns the arising and passing away of things, that is noble and penetrative and leads to the complete destruction of suffering."[54] Since the lay stream-enterer or once-returner is thus well equipped with the wisdom of insight but is not typically described as a jhāna attainer, this implies that attainment of jhāna is not normally expected or required of him. From this we can also conclude that at these early stages of the path liberative wisdom does not depend on a supporting base of jhāna.

(5) A text in the Sotāpatti-saṃyutta gives credit to this conclusion. At SN 55:40/V 398–99, the Buddha explains to the Sakyan Nandiya how a noble disciple dwells diligently (*ariyasāvako appamādavihārī*). He says that a noble disciple should not become complacent about possessing the four factors of stream-entry but should use these qualities as starting points for contemplation: "He is not content with his confirmed confidence in the Buddha (etc.), but strives further in seclusion by day and in retreat by night. As he dwells diligently, gladness arises ... (as above) ... for one who is happy the mind becomes concentrated. When the mind is concentrated, phenomena become manifest. It is with the manifestation of phenomena to him that he is reckoned as 'one who dwells diligently.'"[55]

52. *Saddhā, sīla, suta, cāga, paññā*. Sometimes learning is omitted, since this is not as integral to the *ariyan* character as the other four qualities.

53. See SN 55:32–33, 42–43; V 391–92, 401–2.

54. *Udayatthagāminiyā paññāya samannāgato ariyāya nibbedhikāya sammā-dukkhakkhaya-gāminiyā*.

55. S V 398–99: *Idha Nandiya ariyasāvako Buddhe aveccappasādena samannāgato hoti ... So tena Buddhe aveccappasādena asantuṭṭho uttariṃ vāyamati divā pavivekāya rattiṃ paṭisallānāya. Tassa evaṃ appamattassa viharato pāmujjaṃ jāyati ... sukhino cittaṃ samādhiyati. Samāhite citte dhammā pātubhavanti. Dhammānaṃ pātubhāvā appamādavihārī tveva saṅkhaṃ gacchati.... Evaṃ kho Nandiya ariyasāvako appamādavihārī hoti.*

The expression "manifestation of phenomena" (*dhammānaṃ pātubhāva*) indicates that the disciple is engaged in contemplating the rise and fall of the five aggregates, the six sense bases, and so forth. Thus this passage shows how the disciple proceeds from concentration to insight, but it does not describe this concentration in terms suggesting it occurs at the level of jhāna. Since the sequence switches over from concentration to insight without mentioning jhāna, it seems that the concentration attained will be tantamount to access concentration, not jhāna, yet even this suffices to support the arising of insight.

## 5. When Do the Jhānas Become Necessary?

While there seem to be no suttas that impose an inflexible rule to the effect that a lay noble disciple must possess the jhānas, there are at least two texts that explicitly ascribe all four jhānas to certain householders. One, found in the Citta-saṃyutta (SN 41:9/IV 300–2), features Citta the householder, the foremost lay preacher, in a conversation with a naked ascetic named Kassapa. Kassapa was an old friend of Citta who had embraced the life of renunciation thirty years earlier, and this is apparently their first meeting since that time. Kassapa confesses to Citta that in all these years he has not achieved any "superhuman distinction in knowledge and vision befitting the noble ones" (*uttarimanussadhamma alamariya-ñāṇadassanavisesa*); all he does is go about naked, with a shaved head, using a feather brush to sweep his seat. He then asks Citta whether, as a lay disciple of the Buddha, he has reached any distinguished attainments. Citta says that he has, and then declares his ability to enter and dwell in the four jhānas (he uses the standard formula). To this he adds: "Further, if I were to die before the Blessed One, it would not be surprising if the Blessed One would declare of me: 'There is no fetter bound by which Citta the householder might come back to this world.'"[56] Through this bit of coded text, partly a stock formulation, Citta is informing his friend that he is a non-returner with access to the four jhānas.

---

56. Spk IV 301: *Sace kho pan'āhaṃ bhante Bhagavato paṭhamataraṃ kālaṃ kareyya anacchariyaṃ kho pan'etaṃ yaṃ maṃ Bhagavā etaṃ vyākareyya, Natthi taṃ saññojanaṃ yena saññojanena saṃyutto Citto gahapati puna imaṃ lokaṃ āgaccheyyā ti.*

The other sutta is AN 7:50/A IV 66–67 and concerns the lay woman Nandamātā. In the presence of the Venerable Sāriputta and other monks, Nandamātā has been disclosing the seven wonderful and marvelous qualities with which she is endowed. The sixth of these is possession of the four jhānas, again described by the stock formula. The seventh is as follows: "As to the five lower fetters taught by the Blessed One, I do not see among them any as yet unabandoned in myself."[57] This too is a coded way of declaring her status as a non-returner.

Such are the reports that have come down in the Sutta Piṭaka about two lay followers who possess both the four jhānas and the status of non-returner. Whether these two achievements are inseparably connected or not is difficult to determine on the basis of the Nikāyas, but there are several texts that lend support to this conclusion. One sutta (AN 3:85/A I 231–32) ranks the four classes of noble disciples in relation to the threefold higher training consisting of the higher virtue, the higher mind, and the higher wisdom. Just below, the Buddha explains the training in the higher virtue (*adhisīla-sikkhā*) as the restraint of the Pātimokkha, the code of monastic rules; the training in the higher mind (*adhicitta-sikkhā*), as the four jhānas (defined by the usual formula); and the training in the higher wisdom (*adhipaññā-sikkhā*), as either the knowledge of the four noble truths or liberation from the taints (AN 3:88–89/I 235-36). Although the Buddha's treatment of this topic is governed by a monastic context, the principles of classification can easily be extended to lay disciples. Returning to AN 3:85, we learn that the stream-enterer and the once-returner have fulfilled the training in the higher virtue (which for a lay disciple would mean possession of "the virtues dear to the noble ones") but have accomplished the other two trainings only partly; the non-returner has fulfilled the trainings in the higher virtue and the higher mind but accomplished the training in the higher wisdom only partly; and the arahant has fulfilled all three trainings. Now since the non-returner has fulfilled the training in the higher mind, and this is defined as the four jhānas, he is probably an attainer of the jhānas.

---

57. A IV 67: *Yānīmāni bhante Bhagavatā desitāni panc'orambhāgiyāni saṃyojanāni, nāhaṃ tesaṃ kinci attani appahīnaṃ samanupassāmī ti.*

It might still be questioned, however, whether he must possess all four jhānas. While a literal reading of the above sutta would support this conclusion, if we bear in mind my earlier comments about interpreting stock formulas, we might conjecture that the training in the higher mind is fulfilled by the secure attainment of even one jhāna. This seems to be confirmed by the Mahāmāluṅkya Sutta (MN 64/M I 434-37), which shows how the attainment of jhāna figures in the preliminary phase of the path to the stage of non-returner. At a certain point in his discourse, the Buddha announces that he will teach "the path and way for the abandoning of the five lower fetters" (*yo maggo yā paṭipadā pañcannaṃ orambhāgiyānaṃ saṃyojanānaṃ pahānāya*). He underscores the importance of what he is about to explain with a simile. Just as it is impossible to cut out the heartwood of a great tree without first cutting through the bark and softwood, so it is impossible to cut off the five lower fetters without relying on the path and practice he is about to make known. This lays down categorically that the procedure to be described must be exactly followed to win the promised goal, the eradication of the five lower fetters (the defining achievement of the non-returner).

The Buddha then explains the method. The meditator enters into one of the four jhānas or the lower three formless attainments (the text takes up each in turn) and dissects it into its constituents: form, feeling, perception, volitional formations, and consciousness in the case of the four jhānas; the same, but omitting form, for the three formless attainments.[58] He next contemplates these phenomena in eleven ways: as impermanent, suffering, a disease, a boil, a dart, misery, affliction, alien, disintegrating, empty, and non-self. Then, when his contemplation reaches maturity, he turns his mind away from these things and directs it to the deathless element (*amata-dhātu*), i.e., Nibbāna. "If he is firm in this he reaches arahantship right on the spot, but if he holds back slightly due to attachment and delight in the Dhamma, then he eliminates the five lower fetters

58. According to the commentary, the fourth formless state, the base of neither-perception-nor-non-perception, is not mentioned because its constituents are too subtle to be comprehended by insight. But a parallel text, AN 9:36/A IV 422–26, teaches a method by which the fourth formless attainment, as well as the cessation of feeling and perception, can be used to generate insight and thereby reach arahantship or non-returning.

and becomes a spontaneous ariser, who attains final Nibbāna there (in a celestial realm) without ever returning from that world."[59]

The Mahāmāluṅkya Sutta thus makes the attainment of jhāna a necessary part of the preparatory practice for attaining the stage of non-returner. Though the sutta discusses the practice undertaken by a monk, since the Buddha has declared this to be "the path and practice for abandoning the five lower fetters," we are entitled to infer that lay practitioners too must follow this course. This would imply that a once-returner who aspires to become a non-returner should develop at least the first jhāna in the preliminary phase of the path, using the jhāna as the launching pad for developing insight.

While the Mahāmāluṅkya Sutta and its parallel (AN 9:36/A IV 422–26) imply that prior attainment of the first jhāna is a minimum requirement for reaching the fruit of non-returning, we may still query whether this is an invariable rule or merely a general stipulation that allows for exceptions. Several suttas suggest the latter may in fact be the case. In two consecutive texts the Buddha extols the "eight wonderful and marvelous qualities" of two lay followers named Ugga. In the first (AN 8:21/A IV 211), he declares that Ugga of Vesālī has abandoned all five fetters (as for Nandamātā above); in the second (AN 8:22/A IV 216), he says that Ugga of Hatthigāma has no fetters bound by which he might come back to this world (as for Citta). Yet, though he thus confirms their standing as non-returners, the Buddha does not mention jhānic attainments among their eight wonderful qualities. This, of course, need not be taken to mean that they lacked attainment of jhāna. It may have been that their jhānic skills were less remarkable than the other qualities they possessed, or they may have been adept in only one or two jhānas rather than in all four. But it does leave open the possibility that they were non-returners without jhāna.

Still another suggestive text is the Dīghāvu Sutta (SN 55:3/S V 344–46). Here, the Buddha visits a young lay follower named Dīghāvu, who is gravely ill. He first enjoins the sick boy to acquire confirmed confidence in the Three Jewels and the virtues

59. M I 435–36: *So tatthaṭṭhito āsavānaṃ khayaṃ pāpuṇāti; no ce āsavānaṃ khayaṃ pāpuṇāti ten'eva dhammarāgena tāya dhammanandiyā pancannaṃ orambhāgiyānaṃ saṃyojanānaṃ parikkhayā opapātiko hoti tatthaparinibbāyī anāvattidhammo tasmā lokā.*

dear to the noble ones, that is, to become a stream-enterer. When Dīghāvu declares that he already possesses these qualities, the Buddha tells him that since he is established in the four factors of stream-entry, he should "strive further to develop six qualities that partake of true knowledge" (*cha vijjābhāgiyā dhammā*): "You should dwell contemplating the impermanence of all formations, perceiving suffering in what is impermanent, perceiving non-self in what is suffering, perceiving abandonment, perceiving dispassion, perceiving cessation."[60] Dīghāvu assures the Blessed One that he is already practising these contemplations, and the Master leaves. A short time later Dīghāvu dies. On hearing the news of his death, the monks approach the Buddha to ask about his future rebirth. The Buddha declares that Dīghāvu the lay follower had eradicated the five lower fetters and was spontaneously reborn as a non-returner. Here the transition from stream-entry to non-returning occurs entirely through a series of contemplations that pertain to insight. There has been no exhortation to develop the jhānas, yet through the practice of the "six things partaking of true knowledge" Dīghāvu has severed the five fetters and gained the third fruit of the path.

A theoretical foundation for Dīghāvu's approach might be gleaned from another sutta. At AN 4:169/A II 155–56, the Buddha contrasts two kinds of non-returners: one who attains final Nibbāna without exertion (*asaṅkhāra-parinibbāyī*), and one who attains final Nibbāna with exertion (*sasaṅkhāra-parinibbāyī*). The former is one who enters and dwells in the four jhānas (described by the stock formula). The latter practises instead the "austere" meditations such as the contemplation of the foulness of the body, reflection on the repulsiveness of food, disenchantment with the whole world, perception of impermanence in all formations, and recollection of death.[61] Again, there is no categorical assertion that the latter is altogether bereft of jhāna, but the contrast of this type with one who gains the four jhānas suggests this as a possibility.

60. S V 345: *Cha vijjābhāgiye dhamme uttariṃ bhāveyyāsi. Idha tvaṃ Dīghāvu sabbasaṅkhāresu aniccānupassī viharāhi, anicce dukkhasaññī dukkhe anattasaññī pahānasaññī virāgasaññī nirodhasaññī ti.*

61. A II 156: *Idha bhikkhu asubhānupassī kāye viharati, āhāre paṭikkūlasaññī, sabbaloke anabhiratasaññī, sabbasaṅkhāresu aniccānupassī, maraṇasaññā pan'assa ajjhattaṃ sūpaṭṭhitā hoti.*

Though the possibility that there might be non-returners without jhānas cannot be ruled out, from the Nikāyas we can elicit several reasons why we might normally expect a non-returner to have access to them. One reason is inherent in the very act of becoming a non-returner. In ascending from the stage of once-returner to that of non-returner, the meditator eradicates two fetters that had been merely weakened by the once-returner: sensual desire (*kāmacchanda*) and ill will (*byāpāda*). Now these two fetters are also the first two among the five hindrances, the defilements to be abandoned to gain the jhānas. This suggests that by eradicating these defilements the non-returner permanently removes the main obstacles to concentration. Thus, if his mind so inclines, the non-returner should not find it difficult to enter upon the jhānas.

Another reason why non-returners should be gainers of the jhānas, while stream-enterers and once-returners need not be so, pertains to their future destination in saṃsāra. Though all three types of disciple have escaped the plane of misery—rebirth in hell, the animal realm, and the sphere of ghosts—stream-enterers and once-returners are still liable to rebirth in the sensuous realm (*kāmadhātu*), while non-returners are utterly freed from the prospect of such a rebirth. What keeps the former in bondage to the sensuous realm is the fetter of sensual desire (*kāmacchanda*), which remains inwardly unabandoned by them. If they succeed in attaining the jhānas, they can suppress sensual desire (and the other mental hindrances) and thus achieve rebirth in the form or formless realms. But this is not fixed for noble disciples at the lower two stages, who normally expect only a fortunate rebirth in the human realm or the sense-sphere heavens. Non-returners, on the other hand, are so called precisely because they never again return to the sensuous realm. They have eliminated sensual desire, observe celibacy, and enjoy a high degree of facility in meditation. At death, the non-returner takes rebirth spontaneously in the form realm (generally in the Pure Abodes) and attains final Nibbāna there without ever returning from that world.

The non-returner severs all connection with the sensuous realm by eliminating the fetter of sensual desire, and this establishes a certain correspondence between the non-returner and the ordinary jhāna-attainer. The texts sometimes speak of the worldling jhāna-attainer as "an outsider devoid of lust for sensual pleasures."[62] If he retains mastery over a jhāna at the time of death, his sublime kamma leads him to rebirth in the form realm, the specific plane of rebirth being determined by his degree of mastery over the jhānas. However, while both the ordinary jhāna-attainer and the non-returner are devoid of sensual desire and bound for rebirth in a non-sensuous realm, the two are divided by deep and fundamental differences. The ordinary jhāna-attainer has not fully eliminated any fetters and thus, with a slip of mindfulness, can easily fall victim to sensuality; the non-returner, in contrast, has cut off sensual desire and ill will at the root, ensuring that they will never again arise in him. He is not reborn in the form realm merely through the wholesome kamma generated by the jhānas, like the ordinary jhāna-attainer, but because he has eradicated the two fetters that bind even the once-returner to the sensuous realm.

This difference implies still another difference concerning their long-term fate. The ordinary jhāna-attainer, after being reborn in the form realm, eventually exhausts the powerful meritorious kamma responsible for this sublime rebirth and might then take rebirth in the sensuous realm, even in the nether world. The non-returner, on the other hand, never falls away. Set firmly on the path of the Dhamma, the non-returner who is reborn in the form realm continues to develop the path without ever regressing until he attains final Nibbāna within the form realm itself.[63]

## 6. Conclusions and an Afterthought

Our study has led us to the following conclusions regarding the relationship between lay noble disciples and the jhānas.

(1) Several suttas describe the process by which a worldling enters "the fixed course of rightness" in a way that emphasizes either faith or wisdom as the chief means of attainment. None of the texts, however, that deal with the two candidates for stream-entry—the faith-follower and the Dhamma-follower—show them as being proficient in the jhānas. Though some suttas include the

62. M III 255: *Bāhiraka kāmesu vītarāga.*

63. See AN 4:123/A II 126–28, which contrasts the worldling who attains the jhānas with the Buddhist disciple who attains them.

jhānas in the analysis of the faculty of concentration, this may be done simply out of compliance with the formulaic style of definition employed by the Nikāyas and need not be seen as having categorical implications. The Commentaries treat these definitions as referring to the supramundane jhāna arisen within the supramundane path. Moreover, the analysis of the concentration faculty mentions another type of concentration, which is gained "by making release the object," and this may be interpreted broadly enough as including degrees of concentration short of the jhānas.

(2) All noble disciples acquire the right concentration of the Noble Eightfold Path, which is defined as the four jhānas. This need not be understood to mean that stream-enterers and once-returners already possess jhāna before they reach stream-entry. The formula for right concentration may imply only that they must eventually attain the jhānas in the course of developing the path to its culmination in arahantship. If we go along with the Commentaries in recognizing the Abhidhammic distinction between the preparatory path and the supramundane path, then we can maintain that the jhānas included in right concentration as a path factor pertain to the supramundane path and are thus of supramundane stature. This still leaves open the question whether aspirants for stream-entry must develop the mundane jhānas in the preliminary phase of their practice.

(3) A number of texts on stream-enterers and once-returners imply that they do not possess the jhānas as meditative attainments which they can enter at will. Though it is obvious that disciples at the lower two levels may have jhānic attainments, the latter are not declared to be an integral part of their spiritual equipment.

(4) Several non-returners in the Nikāyas claim to possess all four jhānas, and according to the Mahāmāluṅkya Sutta, attainment of at least the first jhāna is part of the practice leading to the eradication of the five lower fetters. It thus seems likely that stream-enterers and once-returners desirous of advancing to non-returnership in that very same life must attain at least the first jhāna as a basis for developing insight. Those content with their status, prepared to let the "law of the Dhamma" take its course, generally will not strive to attain the jhānas. Instead, they settle for the assurance that they are bound to reach the final goal within a maximum of seven more lives passed in the human and celestial worlds.

(5) As non-returners have eliminated sensual lust and ill will, the main obstacles to jhānic attainment, they should face no major problems in entering the jhānas. The non-returner is similar to the ordinary jhāna-attainer in being bound for rebirth in the form realm. Unlike the latter, however, the non-returner is utterly free from sensual desire and ill will and thus can never fall back to the sensuous realm.

(6) Although in the Nikāyas the tie between the two attainments—the jhānas and non-returnership—is clear enough, it remains an open question whether the connection is absolutely binding. Several suttas speak of the achievements of non-returners without mentioning the jhānas, and at least one sutta contrasts the non-returner who gains all four jhānas with one who practises more austere types of meditation that do not typically lead to the jhānas.

The Commentaries speak even of a *sukkhavipassaka* arahant, an arahant who has gained the goal entirely through "dry insight," without any attainment of form-sphere jhāna at all. Although such a type is not explicitly recognized in the Nikāyas, the question may be raised whether the Commentaries, in asserting the possibility of arahantship without attainment of jhāna in the mundane portion of the path, have deviated from the Canon or brought to light a viable possibility implicit in the older texts. The famous Satipaṭṭhāna Sutta declares, in its conclusion, that all those who earnestly dedicate themselves to uninterrupted practice of the four establishments of mindfulness are bound to reap one of two fruits: either arahantship in this very life or, if any residue of clinging remains, the stage of non-returning. While several exercises within the Satipaṭṭhāna Sutta are certainly capable of inducing the jhānas, the system as a whole seems oriented towards direct insight rather than towards the jhānas.[64] Thus this opens the question whether the Satipaṭṭhāna Sutta might not be propounding a way of practice that leads all the way to non-returning, even to arahantship, without requiring attainment of the jhānas. This, however, is another question, one that lies beyond the scope of this paper.

64. This is a widespread view among contemporary interpreters, though the sutta itself does not describe its method explicitly in such terms.

# What Does Mindfulness Really Mean?

## A Canonical Perspective

### 1. Mindfulness in the Buddhist Path

The entry of systematic mindfulness practice into the fields of stress reduction and psychotherapy has dramatically altered modern medicine's perspectives on our capacity to regulate and overcome our human vulnerabilities. Mindfulness made its debut as a therapeutic discipline in 1979, when Jon Kabat-Zinn introduced his program of "Mindfulness-Based Stress Reduction" at the University of Massachusetts Medical Center. Since then its use to reduce pain and stress has been adopted by hundreds of medical centers, hospitals, and clinics around the world. The application of mindfulness in clinical settings has spread beyond stress reduction to psychotherapy, where it has proven a potent tool for helping patients deal with such conditions as depression, anxiety, and obsessive-compulsive disorders.

While the use of mindfulness for medical purposes may initially seem to be a modern innovation, its roots actually go back twenty-five centuries to the teaching of the Buddha, who lived and taught in northeast India in the fifth century B.C. The Buddha offered his teaching, called the *Dhamma* (Sanskrit *Dharma*), not as a set of doctrines demanding belief but as a body of principles and practices that sustain human beings in their quest for happiness and spiritual freedom. At its heart lies a system of training that leads to insight and the overcoming of suffering. This training spread throughout Asia along with Buddhism itself, and as Buddhism sent down roots in different lands, various lines of meditation flourished in the countries where its teachings were embraced. Many of these lineages have continued down to the present day, preserved in monasteries and hermitages by monks and nuns dedicated to the contemplative life.

In the late 1960s and 1970s, cheaper jet travel facilitated a cultural exchange that would have far-reaching consequences. Asian teachers of Buddhism, yoga, and other spiritual disciplines came to the U.S. and attracted followings of young people disenchanted with materialism, militarism, and the flatlands of modernity. Young westerners also traveled to Asia and studied meditation with Buddhist masters, and then on returning to their home countries began to share what they had learned with their fellow countrymen. As meditation gained in popularity, it caught the attention of medical professionals, neuroscientists, and psychotherapists, setting off an exciting conversation between practitioners of eastern spirituality and western science.

At the heart of all classical systems of Buddhist meditation is a particular discipline that has come to be known as mindfulness. The Buddha himself gave particular prominence to mindfulness by including it in the noble eightfold path, the fourth of the four noble truths into which he compressed his teaching: suffering, its origin, its cessation, and the way leading to its cessation. Right mindfulness (*sammā sati*) is the seventh factor of the path where, wedged between right effort and right concentration, it connects the energetic application of the mind to its stilling and unification.

The Buddha's discourses, as preserved in the Pāli Nikāyas, the early collections, employ a mnemonically terse formulaic style. We thus find right mindfulness consistently defined by a fixed formula that runs as follows:

> "And what, monks, is right mindfulness? Here, a monk dwells contemplating the body in the body, ardent, clearly comprehending, mindful, having removed covetousness and displeasure in regard to the world. He dwells contemplating feelings in feelings ... contemplating mind in mind ... contemplating phenomena in phenomena, ardent, clearly comprehending, mindful, having removed covetousness and displeasure in regard to the world. This is called right mindfulness."[65]

The most influential text in the Pāli Canon on the systematic practice of mindfulness, the Satipaṭṭhāna Sutta, the "Discourse on the Establishment of Mindfulness," opens with a proclamation highlighting both the purpose of this training and its methodology:

65. DN 22.21 (D II 313; LDB 348–49). MN 141.30 (M III 252; MLDB 1100–1101). SN 45:8 (S V 9–10; CDB 1529).

> "Monks, this is the one-way path for the purification of beings, for the overcoming of sorrow and lamentation, for the passing away of pain and displeasure, for the achievement of the method, for the realization of nibbāna, that is, the four establishments of mindfulness. What four? Here, a monk dwells contemplating the body in the body ... feelings in feelings ... mind in mind ... phenomena in phenomena, ardent, clearly comprehending, mindful, having removed covetousness and displeasure in regard to the world. This, monks, is the one-way path for the purification of beings ... for the realization of nibbāna, that is, the four establishments of mindfulness."[66]

In this statement, the Buddha indicates the *goal* of the practice to be the extinction of suffering and the attainment of *nibbāna* (Sanskrit *nirvāṇa*), a state of transcendent bliss and peace. The *method* is the four *satipaṭṭhānas*, the four establishments of mindfulness. From the formula for right mindfulness, we can deduce two important facts about the practice, one pertaining to its objective side, the other to its subjective side. On the objective side, we see that right mindfulness involves the reflexive contemplation of one's own experience, subsumed under the four objective domains of the body, feelings, states of mind, and experiential phenomena. The last of these is, in Pāli, called *dhammā*, a word which we can understand to designate experiential phenomena as organized into certain groups determined by the objectives of the Buddha's teaching, "*the* Dhamma" in the broadest sense.

On the subjective side, the formula shows that the "establishment of mindfulness" involves not only mindfulness but a constellation of mental factors that work in unison. Mindfulness, in the context of *satipaṭṭhāna* practice, always occurs as part of an *anupassanā*, a word that further clarifies its role. We usually translate *anupassanā* as "contemplation," but it might also be illuminating to understand it more literally as an act of "observation." The word is made up of the prefix *anu*, which suggests repetition or closeness, and the base *passanā*, which means "seeing." Thus mindfulness is part of a process that involves a close, repetitive observation of the object.

In the "*satipaṭṭhāna* refrain" several mental factors enter into this *anupassanā*, indicated by the phrase "ardent, clearly comprehending,

---

66. DN 22.1 (D II 290; LDB 335). MN 10.1 (M I 55; MLDB 145).

and mindful" (*ātāpi sampajāno satimā*). Each of these words, according to the classical commentaries, represents a specific mental factor. "Ardent" (*ātāpī*) implies energy, the strength to engage in the practice. Mindfulness (*sati*) is the element of watchfulness, the lucid awareness of each event that presents itself on the successive occasions of experience. The cognitive factor is indicated by the word *sampajāno*, "clearly comprehending," an adjective related to the noun *sampajañña*, "clear comprehension."

The two terms, *sato* and *sampajāno*, often occur in proximity, implying a close affinity between their respective nouns, *sati* or mindfulness and *sampajañña* or clear comprehension. To distinguish the two, I would describe mindfulness as lucid awareness of the phenomenal field. This element of lucid awareness prevails in the initial stages of the practice. But with the strengthening of mindfulness, clear comprehension supervenes and adds the cognitive element. In the practice of insight meditation, the meditator clearly comprehends the nature and qualities of arisen phenomena and relates them to the framework defined by the parameters of the Dhamma, the teaching as an organic whole. The expression "clearly comprehending" thus suggests that the meditator not only observes phenomena but *interprets* the presentational field in a way that sets arisen phenomena in a meaningful context. As the practice advances, clear comprehension takes on an increasingly more important role, eventually evolving into direct insight (*vipassanā*) and wisdom (*paññā*).

## 2. The Meaning of 'sati'

A problem in hermeneutics, with intimate bearings on the actual practice of meditation, concerns the exact meaning of the word *sati* both in general and in relation to Buddhist contemplative activity. We take the rendering "mindfulness" so much for granted that we rarely inquire into the precise nuances of the English term, let alone the meaning of the original Pāli word it represents and the adequacy of the former as a rendering for the latter. The word "mindfulness" is itself so vague and elastic that it serves almost as a cipher into which we can read virtually anything we want. Hence we seldom recognize that the word was chosen as a rendering for *sati* at a particular point in time, after other terms had been tried and found inadequate.

In Indian psychology apart from Buddhism, the word *smṛti*, the Sanskrit equivalent of Pāli *sati*, normally means memory. Thus Monier-Williams, in his *Sanskrit-English Dictionary*, defines *smṛti* as "remembrance, reminiscence, thinking of or upon, calling to mind ... memory."[67] The Buddha's discourses, too, still preserve this meaning in certain contexts, as we will see. But we should not give this excessive importance. When devising a terminology that could convey the salient points and practices of his own teaching, the Buddha inevitably had to draw on the vocabulary available to him. To designate the practice that became the main pillar of his meditative system, he chose the word *sati*. But here *sati* no longer means memory. Rather, the Buddha assigned the word a new meaning consonant with his own system of psychology and meditation. Thus it would be a fundamental mistake to insist on reading the old meaning of memory into the new context.

It would not be a mistake, however, to try to determine how the word *sati* acquired its new application on the basis of the older meaning. Unfortunately for us, the Nikāyas or early discourse collections don't formally define *sati* in the clear expository manner that we are accustomed to find in modern textbooks or in scholarly studies of meditation practice. For four centuries, the Buddhist scriptures were preserved and transmitted orally, from one generation of reciters to the next. This method of transmission required that the compilers of the Buddha's discourses compress the main points into simple repetitive formulas that were conducive to easy memorization. Thus when we consult the texts to find out what they mean by *sati*, what we mostly encounter, instead of lucid explanations, are *operational demonstrations* that indicate, in practical terms, how *sati* functions in Buddhist psychology and meditation practice. It is from these that we must tease out the word's implications, testing them against each other and evaluating them by personal reflection and experience.

The first scholar, it seems, to render *sati* as "mindfulness" was the great British translator T.W. Rhys Davids, founder of the Pali Text Society. His comment in the introduction to his translation of the Mahāsatipaṭṭhāna Sutta still shows remarkable acumen:

---

67. Monier-Williams (2005), p. 1272.

> Etymologically Sati is Memory. But as happened at the rise of Buddhism to so many other expressions in common use, a new connotation was then attached to the word, a connotation that gave a new meaning to it, and renders "memory" a most inadequate and misleading translation. It became the memory, recollection, calling-to-mind, being-aware-of, certain specified facts. Of these the most important was the impermanence (the coming to be as the result of a cause, and the passing away again) of all phenomena, bodily and mental. And it included the repeated application of this awareness, to each experience of life, from the ethical point of view.[68]

The Nikāyas employ two recurrent formulas to illustrate the meaning of *sati*. One harkens back to the old meaning of memory; the other refers to its occurrence in relation to the four *satipaṭṭhānas*. We meet the first in SN 48:9, which provides an analysis of the five spiritual faculties: faith, energy, mindfulness, concentration, and wisdom. The sutta briefly defines each with a short formula, the "faculty of mindfulness" (*satindriya*) as follows:

> "And what, monks, is the faculty of mindfulness? Here, the noble disciple is mindful, possessing supreme mindfulness and alertness, one who remembers and recollects what was done and said long ago. This is called the faculty of mindfulness."[69]

The operative expression in Pāli here is *saritā anussaritā*, "one who remembers and recollects." Both words are agent nouns derived from the verb *sarati*, "to remember" or "to be mindful"; the first is simple, the second is prefixed with *anu*. While the two words, taken in isolation, might be interpreted as referring either to remembrance or mindfulness, the phrase "what was done and said long ago" (*cirakatampi cirabhāsitampi*) favors interpreting *sati* here in terms of memory.

---

68. Rhys Davids 1910: 322.

69. S V 197 (CDB 1671). The formula also occurs at AN 5:14 (A III 11; NDB 637) and AN 7:4 (A IV 4; NDB 999) as a definition of the "power of mindfulness." Interestingly, the Chinese parallels to SN 48:9 (SĀ 646 at T II 182b19) and AN 5:14 (SĀ 675 at T II 185c12) define the faculty and power of mindfulness, respectively, by way of the four bases of mindfulness. This might have resulted from standardization made at a time when the old meaning of memory had faded even further into the background.

However, in the next sutta, SN 48:10, the five faculties are defined again. The faculty of mindfulness is first defined as in the preceding sutta, as the ability to recollect what was done and said long ago. But then, as if admitting that this definition is inadequate, the text adds the stock formula on the four establishments of mindfulness: "He dwells contemplating the body in the body ... phenomena in phenomena, ardent, clearly comprehending, mindful, having removed covetousness and displeasure in regard to the world. This is called the faculty of mindfulness."[70] This indicates that the compilers of the texts weren't satisfied with the simple definition in terms of memory but felt the need to supplement it with another definition that underscores its connection with meditation practice. The next sutta, SN 48:11, raises the question: "What is the faculty of mindfulness?" and answers: "The mindfulness that one obtains on the basis of the four establishments of mindfulness: this is called the faculty of mindfulness."[71] Here, *sati* as memory isn't brought in at all. One might suggest that *sati* as mindfulness, in the sense of a lucid awareness of the present, enables *sati* to function as memory. While this may be factually true, the texts themselves make no such suggestion but simply juxtapose the two formulations without explanation.

We find this ambivalence in the meaning of *sati* emerge from two otherwise parallel expositions on the seven factors of enlightenment (*satta bojjhaṅga*). The first enlightenment factor is mindfulness (*satisambojjhaṅga*), which is followed in order by investigation, energy, joy, tranquility, concentration, and equanimity. The earlier sutta, SN 46:3, opens with the Buddha praising the benefits of associating with monks fully accomplished in the training, one benefit being that a monk gets to hear the Dhamma from them. Having heard the Dhamma from them, "the monk recollects that Dhamma and thinks it over. By doing so, on that occasion the monk arouses, develops, and fulfills the enlightenment factor of mindfulness."[72] In this passage, invisible in the English translation, mindfulness (*sati*) as an enlightenment factor is derived from the act of recollecting and reflecting on the teaching one has heard.

70. S V 198 (CDB 1672).
71. S V 200 (CDB 1673).
72. S V 67 (CDB 1571).

The two verbs used are *anussarati* and *anuvitakketi*. The first is an augmented form of *sarati*, "to remember," from which the noun *sati* is derived; the second is the basis for the noun *vitakka*, thought or reflection. The discourse continues through the other six factors of enlightenment and ends with the fruits of the practice.

Taken on its own, this text seems to reinforce the interpretation of *sati* as the exercise of memory. However, in another sutta, SN 54:13, the Buddha treats each of the four establishments of mindfulness as a springboard to the seven factors of enlightenment. And so, when a monk "dwells contemplating the body in the body ... phenomena in phenomena, on that occasion the monk arouses, develops, and fulfills the enlightenment factor of mindfulness."[73] Once mindfulness has arisen, the other factors of enlightenment arise in turn, culminating in "true knowledge and liberation." This text has the same scaffolding as the earlier one, but here the enlightenment factor of mindfulness emerges *not* from memory, *not* from recollecting teachings that one has heard, but from direct contemplation of the body, feelings, mind, and experiential phenomena.

There is one Pāli word used by the commentaries to clarify the meaning of *sati* which, I think, testifies to an attempt to underscore the new role being assigned to it. This word is *upaṭṭhāna*. *Upaṭṭhāna* means, firstly, "setting up, establishing," which is what one does with mindfulness. Already in the Nikāyas the word is closely connected with *sati*. The compound *satipaṭṭhāna* is itself composed of *sati* and *upaṭṭhāna*. The four *satipaṭṭhānas* are the four *establishments* of mindfulness, a process *of setting up* mindfulness, distinguished as fourfold by way of its objective domains. This analysis indicates that to establish mindfulness is not to set about remembering something that occurred in the past, but to adopt a particular stance towards one's present experience. I characterize this as a stance of *observation* or *watchfulness* towards one's own experience. One might even call the stance of *sati* a "bending back" of the light of consciousness upon the experiencing subject in its physical, sensory, and psychological dimensions. This act of "bending back" serves to illuminate the events occurring in these domains, lifting them out from the twilight zone of unawareness into the light of clear cognition.

73. S V 329–33 (CDB 1780–85).

The sense of "presence" pertaining to the word *upaṭṭhāna* comes out more explicitly in a canonical exegetical work called the *Paṭisambhidāmagga*, which glosses each of the five faculties with another term through which it is to be "directly known" (*abhiññeyyaṃ*). Thus the faculty of faith is to be directly known as conviction; the faculty of energy, as exertion; the faculty of mindfulness, as presence (*upaṭṭhānaṭṭhena satindriyaṃ*); the faculty of concentration, as non-distraction; and the faculty of wisdom, as seeing.[74] Here, *sati* is equated with *upaṭṭhāna* not in the sense that the meditator "establishes mindfulness," but in the sense that mindfulness is itself an act of establishing presence. Mindfulness establishes the presence of the object and thereby makes it available to scrutiny and discernment.

This interpretation brings out the impact the practice of *sati* has on its objective field. On the one hand, we might say that it brackets the "objectification" of the object that occurs in our everyday interactions with the world, whereby we treat objects as things "out there" subservient to our pragmatic purposes. On the other hand, *sati* makes the objective field "present" to awareness as an expanse of phenomena exhibiting their own distinctive phenomenal characteristics as well as patterns and structures common to all conditioned phenomena. The net effect is to make the objective field clearly available for inspection. The *Visuddhimagga* supports this hypothesis when it states that *sati* has as its manifestation "directly facing the objective domain" (*visayābhimukhabhāvapaccupaṭṭhānā*).[75] We might characterize mindfulness in this sense, in the simplest terms, as *lucid awareness*.[76]

I believe it is this aspect of *sati* that provides the connection between its two primary canonical meanings: as memory and as lucid awareness of present happenings. *Sati* makes the apprehended

---

74. Paṭis I 20. Though included in the Pāli Canon, the *Paṭisambhidāmagga* obviously dates from a period later than the old Nikāyas, which contain the Buddha's discourses. The work was a major influence on the *Visuddhimagga*, which often quotes from it.

75. Vism 464, Ch. 14.141.

76. I hesitate to use the word "awareness" without qualification as a rendering of *sati*, for this word has been chosen to represent a number of Pāli technical terms ranging from *viññāṇa* (consciousness) and *citta* (mind) to *sati*, *sampajañña*, and *vijjā* (penetrative knowledge).

object stand forth vividly and distinctly before the mind. When the object being cognized pertains to the past—when it is apprehended as something that was formerly done, perceived, or spoken—its vivid presentation takes the form of memory. When the object is a bodily process like in-and-out breathing or the act of walking back and forth, or when it is a mental event like a feeling or thought, its vivid presentation takes the form of lucid awareness of the present.

In the Pāli suttas, *sati* has still other roles in relation to meditation but these reinforce its characterization in terms of lucid awareness and vivid presentation. For example, the texts include as types of mindfulness recollection of the Buddha (*buddhānussati*), contemplation of the repulsiveness of the body (*asubhasaññā*), and mindfulness of death (*maraṇasati*); for each brings its objective domain vividly before the mind. The Metta Sutta even refers to meditation on loving-kindness as a kind of mindfulness.[77] In each of these cases, the object is a conceptual phenomenon—the qualities of the Buddha, the repulsiveness of the body, the inevitability of death, or lovable living beings—yet the mental pose that attends to them is designated mindfulness. What unites them, from the side of the subject, is the lucidity and vivacity of the act of awareness, and from the side of the object, its vivid presentation.

Apart from the meditative context, *sati* enters the noble eightfold path in another role that cannot be overlooked if we are to determine its exact meaning. This is as a guarantor of the correct practice of all the other path factors. MN 117 draws distinctions between the wrong (*micchā*) and right (*sammā*) versions of the first five path factors, from views to livelihood. After making each distinction, it then explains how right view, right effort, and right mindfulness occur in association with each path factor. Taking right intention as an example, the text reads: "One understands wrong intention as it is and right intention as it is; this is one's right view.... One makes an effort to abandon wrong intention and to acquire right intention: this is one's right effort. Mindfully one abandons

77. Recollection of the Buddha is at AN 6:10 (A III 285–288; NDB 862–65), AN 6:25 (A III 312–14; NDB 883–84), etc. Contemplation of the body's repulsiveness is at DN 22.5 (LDB 337) and MN 10.10 (MLDB 147) and elsewhere. Mindfulness of death is at AN 6:19 and AN 6:20 (A III 303–308; NDB 876–880). Sn 151 says about meditation on loving-kindness: *etaṃ satiṃ adhiṭṭheyya*, "one should resolve on this mindfulness."

wrong intention and mindfully one acquires and dwells in right intention: this is one's right mindfulness."[78] The same stipulation is laid down with regard to the other factors, including right speech, right action, and right livelihood, thus ensuring that one mindfully embraces the ethical constituents of the path.

This explanation makes problematic the common interpretation of mindfulness as a type of awareness intrinsically devoid of discrimination, evaluation, and judgment. While such a depiction of mindfulness has gained currency in the popular literature on meditation, it does not square well with the canonical texts and may even lead to a distorted view of how mindfulness is to be practiced. There are certainly occasions when the cultivation of mindfulness requires the practitioner to suspend discrimination, evaluation, and judgment, and to adopt instead a stance of simple observation. However, to fulfill its role as an *integral* member of the eightfold path mindfulness has to work in unison with right view and right effort. This means that the practitioner of mindfulness must at times evaluate mental qualities and intended deeds, make judgments about them, and engage in purposeful action. In conjunction with right view, mindfulness enables the practitioner to distinguish wholesome qualities from unwholesome ones, good deeds from bad deeds, beneficial states of mind from harmful states. In conjunction with right effort, it promotes the removal of unwholesome mental qualities and the acquisition of wholesome qualities. It is only in this way that the practice of mindfulness can lay a foundation for correct wisdom to arise and extirpate the roots of suffering.

## 3. Mindfulness and Bare Attention

Many commentators who teach and practice in the contemporary vipassana movement have sought to convey the experiential flavor of mindfulness by means of the expression "bare attention." With certain reservations (which I will discuss below), I believe this characterization is acceptable if understood as a *procedural directive* for cultivating mindfulness in accordance with certain methods. It helps a novice meditator who has newly embarked on this unfamiliar enterprise get a grip on the appropriate way to observe

78. MN 117.10–15 (M III 72–73; MLDB 935–36).

the phenomenal field. The purpose of the expression would then be seen as pragmatic rather than doctrinal, as pedagogical rather than definitive.

When, however, it is considered in the light of canonical sources, it is hard to see "bare attention" as a valid *theoretical* description of mindfulness applicable to all its modalities. As I showed earlier, mindfulness is a versatile mental quality that can be developed in a variety of ways. While certain methods emphasize a type of awareness that might be pragmatically described as "bare attention," in the full spectrum of Buddhist meditation techniques this is only one among a number of alternative ways to cultivate mindfulness many of which are not shy about utilizing conceptual thought and an explicit scheme of values. We saw above that mindfulness can be developed by attending to the repulsiveness of the body, contemplating death, and pervading beings with loving-kindness. What unites all these—as well as bare attention—is a quality of lucid awareness that allows the object to stand forth with a vivid and distinct presence.

A further problem that arises when the expression "bare attention" is taken to be more than a pedagogical device is that it involves a crossing of technical terms that in a rigorous deployment of Buddhist terminology should be kept apart. One influential attempt to establish a theoretical equivalency between mindfulness and "bare attention" is a passage in Ven. Henepola Gunaratana's popular book, *Mindfulness in Plain English*, often cited on the internet. Here we find mindfulness identified with the brief moment of preconceptual awareness that, in Buddhist cognitive theory, precedes the onset of conceptual determination:

> When you first become aware of something, there is a fleeting instant of pure awareness just before you conceptualize the thing, before you identify it. That is a state of awareness. Ordinarily, this state is short-lived. It is that flashing split second just as you focus your eyes on the thing, just as you focus your mind on the thing, just before you objectify it, clamp down on it mentally, and segregate it from the rest of existence. It takes place just before you start thinking about it—before your mind says, "Oh, it's a dog." *That flowing, soft-focused moment of pure awareness is mindfulness....* That original moment of mindfulness is rapidly

passed over. It is the purpose of vipassana meditation to train us to prolong that moment of awareness.[79]

A little later, the author emphasizes the non-conceptual, non-discursive quality of mindfulness, which he explicitly identifies with bare attention:

> Mindfulness is nonconceptual awareness. Another English term for sati is "bare attention." It is not thinking. It does not get involved with thought or concepts.... It is, rather, the direct and immediate experiencing of whatever is happening, without the medium of thought. It comes before thought in the perceptual process.[80]

These passages seem to conflate two mental functions that, in classical Buddhist accounts of cognition, are regarded as distinct. One is the immediate preconceptual apprehension of an object that occurs as soon as the object comes into range of cognition. This act occurs automatically and spontaneously. It is ethically indeterminate, common to the thief and the saint, the toddler and the thinker, the sensualist and the yogi. Mindfulness, in contrast, does not occur automatically but is a quality to be cultivated (*bhāvetabba*). It arises when the cognitive processing of the object is already well underway and, far from being spontaneous, comes into being through a deliberate effort. It also has an ethical function, being part and parcel of the attempt to eliminate the unwholesome and establish the wholesome.

Since mindfulness plays the key role in such meditations as recollection of the Buddha, the perception of the body's repulsiveness, and mindfulness of death, it is also hard to see how mindfulness can be essentially non-conceptual and non-discursive. In certain types of mindfulness practice, conceptualization and discursive thought may be suspended in favor of non-conceptual observation, but there is little evidence in the Pāli Canon and its commentaries that mindfulness *by its very nature* is devoid of conceptualization. In some types of mindfulness practice emphasis falls on simple observation of what is occurring in the present, in others less so.

79. Gunaratana 2002: 138. Italics mine.

80. *Ibid.*, p. 140.

Even in the simple observational stance, there is a dichotomy in how mindfulness is applied. Mindfulness may be focused on a single point of observation, as in mindfulness of breathing, especially when developed for the purpose of attaining concentration (*samādhi*). But mindfulness may also be open and undirected, accessing whatever phenomena appear, especially when applied for the purpose of developing insight (*vipassanā*). Still other types of mindfulness practice make extensive use of conceptualization and discursive thought, but apply them in a different way than in ordinary thinking. Instead of allowing thought to drift at random, governed by defiled emotions, habit patterns, and practical survival needs, the meditator deliberately uses thought and concepts to keep the object before the mind.

To my knowledge, the first person to use the expression "bare attention" to characterize mindfulness was the elder German monk, Ven. Nyanaponika Thera, my own spiritual teacher with whom I lived for twelve years at his hermitage in Sri Lanka. Nyanaponika was also probably the first Western writer on Buddhism to explore the practice of mindfulness at length, which he did both in his influential book, *The Heart of Buddhist Meditation*, and in his tract, *The Power of Mindfulness*. Nyanaponika did not intend "bare attention" to be a translation of *sati* (he used the established rendering "mindfulness"), but coined the term to highlight the initial stage in the practice of *satipaṭṭhāna*. To distinguish the two components of the practice, *sati* and *sampajañña*, he wrote that "mindfulness (*sati*) applies preeminently to the attitude and practice of bare attention in a purely receptive state of mind [while] clear comprehension (*sampajañña*) comes into operation when any kind of action is required, including active reflective thoughts on things observed."[81] I will have more to say about clear comprehension below. For now I am concerned with bare attention.

Nyanaponika defines bare attention quite succinctly thus:

> Bare attention is the clear and single-minded awareness of what actually happens to us and in us, at the successive moments of perception. It is called "bare" because it attends just to the bare facts of a perception as presented either through the five

81. Nyanaponika 1962: 29. Here and below I take the liberty of lower casing the first letters of Buddhist technical terms that Nyanaponika, following German custom, capitalized.

physical senses or through the mind ... When attending to that sixfold sense impression, attention or mindfulness is kept to a bare registering of the facts observed, without reacting to them by deed, speech, or by mental comment, which may be one of self-reference (like, dislike, etc.), judgement or reflection.[82]

Contrary to some contemporary vipassana teachers, Nyanaponika did not regard "bare attention" as non-conceptual and non-verbal. The Mahasi Sayadaw system of insight meditation, which he had practiced, stresses the importance of precisely labeling the constituents of one's experience, and Nyanaponika developed this methodology in his own way informed by keen psychological acumen. Although he highlights the open, receptive, and non-judgmental attitude inherent in bare attention, he also held that precise verbal designation plays a critical role in the three tasks of knowing, shaping, and purifying the mind.

In *The Power of Mindfulness* Nyanaponika calls this process "tidying up the mental household."[83]He writes that this work requires us to examine the mind's "dark, untidy corners," which are "the hideouts of our most dangerous enemies," the mental defilements of greed, hate, and delusion. Such examination is the work of mindfulness as bare attention, which involves calling things by their true names:

> The calmly observant glance of mindfulness discovers the demons in their hiding-places. The practice of calling them by their names drives them out into the open, into the daylight of consciousness. There they will feel embarrassed and obliged to justify themselves, although at this stage of bare attention they have not yet even been subjected to any closer questioning except about their names, their identity. If forced into the open while still in an incipient stage, they will be incapable of withstanding scrutiny and will just dwindle away. Thus a first victory over them may be won, even at an early stage of the practice.[84]

---

82. *Ibid.*, p. 30. An almost identical definition is found in Nyanaponika 1968: 3.
83. *Ibid.*, p. 1.
84. *Ibid.*, p. 8.

Although I see significant differences between Nyanaponika's interpretation of mindfulness and interpretations in popular presentations of meditation, I still believe it was a mistake for him to use the expression "bare attention" to describe this preliminary stage of mindfulness. I make this claim for two reasons, one pertaining to the word "attention," the other to the word "bare."

My reservation regarding "attention" derives from the use of this word as the standard rendering for another technical term in the Buddhist analysis of mind, *manasikāra*, which designates a mental function whose role is quite different from that of mindfulness. The principal role of *manasikāra* is to turn the mind to an object. It is a spontaneous and automatic function exercised whenever an object impinges on a sense faculty or arises at the "mind door." It is translated "attention" in the sense that it is the turning of attention to an object, the mind's "advertence to the object."[85] This, however, is not the role of *sati*. By explaining *sati*, even in its rudimentary stage, as "bare attention," Nyanaponika merged its meaning with that of *manasikāra*. But whereas *manasikāra* generally predominates at the inception of a cognitive process, *sati* supervenes at a later stage, sustaining attention on the object and making it appear vividly to lucid cognition.

Nyanaponika was a keen scholar of the Buddhist psychological system known as Abhidhamma and thus his choice of "attention" to characterize *sati* could not have been due to carelessness. I suspect that the underlying reason for his choice was a melding of words in the two European languages in which he wrote, German and English. In his earliest works, written in German, he had rendered *sati* as *achtsamkeit*, which means "attentiveness, heedfulness, ... mindfulness, care."[86] Thus, whereas "mindfulness" might be regarded as synonymous with "attentiveness" in the sense of sustained attention, when it is glossed as "bare attention" this risks confounding *sati* and *manasikāra*, deliberate mindfulness and the automatic act

85. *Manasikāra* also occurs in another context, when it is prefixed either by *ayoniso* or *yoniso*. *Ayoniso manasikāra* is "careless reflection," attending to an object in a way that causes unarisen defilements to arise and arisen defilements to increase. *Yoniso manasikāra* is the opposite: careful reflection on an object that prevents unarisen defilements from arising and removes arisen defilements.

86. See http://en.bab.la/dictionary/german-english/achtsamkeit.

of advertence. I think it was this conflation of the two technical terms that led Gunaratana, in the passage cited above, to identify mindfulness with the brief moment of non-conceptual awareness that precedes the arising of concepts and discursive thought.

My reservation about using the word "bare" to qualify this type of attention rests on more philosophical grounds. I think the expression "bare attention" can be pragmatically useful to guide a beginning practitioner in the method of setting up mindfulness, and this is presumably what Nyanaponika had in mind when he wrote that bare attention "is kept to a bare registering of the facts observed, without reacting to them by deed, speech, or by mental comment." However, from a theoretical perspective it is questionable whether any act of attention, or any other mental act, can literally be "bare." As I see it, virtually any intentional act is necessarily subject to a vast set of determinants, internal and external, that governs the way it functions. It occurs *embodied* in a particular person with a unique biography and personality, and it occurs *embedded* in a particular context—historical, social, and cultural—that gives it a specific orientation on which its very identity depends.

We can, for example, distinguish contextual orientations depending on whether the practice is taken up by a traditional Buddhist who subscribes to the classical Buddhist worldview or by a contemporary westerner who takes up meditation against the background of a holistic secular perspective. The difference is neatly summarized by Gil Fronsdal:

> Rather than stressing world-renunciation, they [Western lay teachers] stress engagement with, and freedom within the world. Rather than rejecting the body, these Western teachers embrace the body as part of the wholistic [sic] field of practice. Rather than stressing ultimate spiritual goals such as full enlightenment, ending the cycles of rebirth, or attaining the various stages of sainthood, many Western teachers tend to stress the immediate benefits of mindfulness and untroubled, equanimous presence in the midst of life's vicissitudes.[87]

Surely these differences in orientation are going to flow over and shape the experience of mindfulness. One might argue that

87. Gil Fronsdal 1995.

awareness of the breath is awareness of the breath no matter who is breathing. While I certainly could not dispute this, I also think it likely that once a meditator goes beyond this preliminary stage, presuppositions and expectations will inevitably come into play.

Instead of thinking of mindfulness as being exclusively "bare," I prefer to think of it as spread out along a spectrum, with varying layers of conceptual content ranging from "heavy" to "light" to "zero," depending on the particular style of mindfulness being practiced. Even the *satipaṭṭhāna* system itself shows such variation. In certain *satipaṭṭhāna* exercises, the determining context and orientation might be "heavy," in others "light." For example, in contemplation of the repulsiveness of the body, attention to the four elements, or the charnel ground meditations, the orientation towards disenchantment and dispassion is heavily loaded from the start. From the outset, mindfulness works in close association with thought and examination (*vitakka* and *vicāra*), which requires a sophisticated deployment of conceptual activity. The style of insight meditation taught by Mahasi Sayadaw makes much lighter use of conceptualization. A meditator begins by merely noting the expansion and contraction of the abdomen, and then gradually extends the act of noting to anything that impinges on awareness.[88] In a system that aims at the attainment of the jhānas, the conceptual content will be much thinner and effectively vanish with the actual attainment of jhāna, even while mindfulness becomes purer and clearer.

But in all cases, if mindfulness is to qualify as the "right mindfulness" (*sammā sati*) of the noble eightfold path, it will have to be connected to a web of factors that give it direction and purpose. As a component of the path, it must be guided by right view, the first path factor, which links the practice to understanding. It must be directed by right intention, the second factor, the aspiration for dispassion, benevolence, and harmlessness. It should be grounded in the three ethical factors of right speech, right action, and right livelihood. And it should be conjoined with right effort (*sammā vāyāma*), the endeavor to eliminate unwholesome mental qualities and to awaken and fulfill wholesome qualities.

In short, the expression "bare attention" seems faulty in two respects: first, because it conflates the two distinct mental factors of

88. See Mahasi Sayadaw 1971: 3–12.

*sati* and *manasikāra*; and second, because no act of cognition is ever entirely devoid of factors imparting to it orientation and meaning. In relation to *satipaṭṭhāna* practice, one might perhaps speak of different degrees of coloring, different "weights" of a determining context. However, I don't believe one can ever leave behind all determinants and achieve a state of absolute openness, vacuity, and indeterminacy.

## 4. What the Suttas Say

Nevertheless, despite my reservations about the use of "bare attention" as an alternative expression for *sati*, if we consider *how* mindfulness is to be practiced in the system laid down in the Satipaṭṭhāna Sutta, we can find considerable support for the idea that the initial task of *sati* is to "keep to a bare registering of the facts observed" as free as possible from *distorting* conceptual elaborations. The problem, as I see it, is not with conceptualization itself, but with conceptualization that ascribes erroneous attributes to the objects and the experiential act itself. An experiential event can be viewed as a field distributed between two poles, the objective datum and the subjective act that cognizes it. Ordinarily, on account of the spontaneous functioning of unenlightened consciousness, this polarity is reified into a sharp duality of subject and object. The subjective pole seems to coalesce into a substantially existent "I," an ego-self that hovers in the background as an autonomous and independent entity. The objective pole presents itself as an object that is there "for me," ready to serve or oppose my purposes; thus it becomes a potential object of craving or aversion. This process is what the suttas refer to as "I-making" and "mine-making" (*ahaṃkāra mamaṃkāra*). It is the task of meditation to dismantle this structure by penetrating the selfless nature of all phenomena, whether pertaining to the objective or subjective poles of the experience.

While it is only *paññā* or wisdom that can eradicate the cognitive distortions, *sati* helps to keep them in check. By bringing into focus the experiential field, *sati* illuminates objects without the usual overlay of distorted conceptual elaborations that obscure their real nature. The initial instruction on mindfulness of breathing, the first exercise in contemplation of the body, exemplifies this well. The meditator sits down, holds his body erect, and establishes mindfulness in front of him. Then, "just mindful he breathes in, mindful he breathes out" (*sato va assasati, sato passasati*). The expression *sato va* is emphatic: *just* mindful, *only* mindful, *simply* mindful. Here, contrary to its original sense, *sati* could not mean "remembering." The only thing the meditator should be remembering is to keep the breath in mind. The breath is something occurring in the present, not in the past, which means that in this context *sati* is attentiveness to a present event, not recollection of the past.

The instruction continues: "When a monk breathes in long, he knows, 'I breathe in long'; and when he breathes out long, he knows, 'I breathe out long.'" The same is said with regard to short breaths. The key word here is *pajānāti*, "one knows." The verb is the source of the noun *paññā*, usually translated "wisdom," but it is clear that at this point *paññā* as wisdom has not yet arisen. What occurs, rather, is just a simple, even minimal, discernment of the quality of the breath. We might see two phases to be involved in this process. First, mindfulness, as the quality of *upaṭṭhāna* or lucid awareness, illuminates the presence of the breath. Then, almost simultaneously, a simple cognition, indicated by *pajānāti*, steps in and registers the breath as coming in or going out, as long or short. We can see this as a rudimentary act of *sampajañña*, clear comprehension.

The same method of description is found in the sections on feelings and states of mind. When the meditator experiences a particular feeling—pleasant, painful, or neutral—he knows what he feels. When a particular state of mind has arisen—a mind with lust, hatred, or delusion, or a mind without lust, hatred, or delusion—in each case he knows that state of mind just as it is. As I see it, in such contemplation, the role of *sati* or mindfulness is to lay open the contents of the experiential field; the role of *sampajañña*, clear comprehension, is to determine and define the contents for what they are. *Sampajañña* advances and begins to turn into *paññā* in the section on contemplating the arising and vanishing of each type of object. This act explicitly relates them to the broad scheme set up by the teachings.

With the fourth contemplation, contemplation of phenomena (*dhammānupassanā*), the situation becomes more complex and thus clear comprehension gains prominence. The first division of this section deals with the five hindrances: sensual desire, ill will, drowsiness, restlessness, and doubt. Once again mindfulness lays open the experiential field and clear comprehension recognizes the presence or absence of a particular hindrance. When mindfulness and clear comprehension have jointly exercised this preparatory function, *paññā*, in the sense of wisdom, enters and subsumes the hindrance under the principle of conditionality. The meditator must understand how the hindrance arises, how it is abandoned, and how it can be prevented from arising again in the future.

A similar sequence is found in the following exercises on the five aggregates, the six inner and outer sense bases, the seven enlightenment factors, and the four noble truths. In each case, considerably more is involved than "bare attention" to the flux of immediate experience. Rather, investigation is needed in order to understand how certain factors arise, how they are eliminated or strengthened, and in the case of the positive factors, how they are brought to fulfillment. As a matter of necessity, one adopts certain conceptual schemes as matrices through which to view the vortex of experience, schemes that plot phenomena against the guidelines mandated by the Dhamma and steer the practice towards its intended goal, the realization of *nibbāna*. At this point the direction, context, and orientation of the practice, far from being dispensable, have a decisive impact on the way mindfulness operates.

## 5. Clear Comprehension

While I said just above that clear comprehension plays a more prominent role in the contemplation of experiential phenomena, the refrain on right mindfulness shows that clear comprehension has been present to some degree all along. The formula describes clear comprehension as a constant entering each exercise virtually from the start. Whether contemplating the body, feelings, states of mind, or experiential phenomena, the meditator dwells "ardent, clearly comprehending, and mindful."

In the Nikāyas, there are two stock passages that describe the practice of clear comprehension. The more frequent passage occurs as a separate section in the Satipaṭṭhāna Sutta, comprised under contemplation of the body:

> "And how, monks, does a monk exercise clear comprehension? Here, a monk acts with clear comprehension when

> going forward and returning; when looking ahead and looking aside; when drawing in and extending the limbs; when wearing his robes and carrying his outer robe and bowl; when eating, drinking, chewing his food, and tasting; when defecating and urinating; when walking, standing, sitting, falling asleep, waking up, speaking, and keeping silent. It is in such a way that a monk exercises clear comprehension."[89]

Taken in isolation, this account might give the impression that clear comprehension refers solely to the deliberative performance of one's daily tasks. However, a pair of suttas addressed to sick monks in the infirmary shows that mindfulness and clear comprehension jointly lead to insight and liberation. On two separate occasions the Buddha visits the infirmary and enjoins the monks to be mindful and clearly comprehend things. He explains the former by way of the stock formula on the four *satipaṭṭhānas* and the latter by the above formula on clear comprehension. He then states that a monk who is mindful and clearly comprehends things will understand the dependent origination of feelings, contemplate their impermanence, and abandon lust, aversion, and ignorance, whereby he attains nibbāna.[90]

The other passage on clear comprehension has a different emphasis. It describes clear comprehension, not as discernment of one's day-to-day activities, but as a reflexive cognition of mental events:

> "And how does a monk exercise clear comprehension? Here, for a monk feelings are understood as they arise, as they remain present, as they pass away. Thoughts are understood as they arise, as they remain present, as they pass away. Perceptions are understood as they arise, as they remain present, as they pass away. It is in this way that a monk exercises clear comprehension."[91]

---

89. DN 22.4 (D II 292; LDB 337). MN 10.8 (M I 57; MLDB 147). The same passage occurs in many discourses on the "progressive training." See, e.g., DN 2.65 (D I 70–71; LDB 100); MN 27.16 (M I 181; MLDB 274); AN 4:198 (A II 210; NDB 584).

90. SN 36.7, 36.8 (S IV 210–14; CDB 1266–69).

91. SN 47:35 (S V 180–81; CDB 1657). See too AN 4:41 (A II 45; NDB 431–32), which calls this the development of concentration that leads to mindfulness and clear comprehension.

This stage of contemplation evidently marks a turning point where *sampajañña* is maturing into *paññā*, where clear comprehension becomes insight into impermanence, direct knowledge of the arising and passing of phenomena.

The Pāli commentaries consistently explain clear comprehension to have a fourfold application: (1) as comprehending the purpose of one's actions; (2) as prudence in the choice of means; (3) as engagement with the meditation subject; and (4) as discernment of things in their true nature. We might correlate the first two applications with clear comprehension in one's daily tasks, as described in the first formula. The third might be interpreted as the clear comprehension referred to by the word *sampajāno* in the *satipaṭṭhāna* refrain. And the fourth obviously marks the stage where clear comprehension turns into actual insight.[92]

## 6. EXPANDING INTO NEW FRONTIERS

Mindfulness has traveled a long way from its homeland in northeast India. It has journeyed to the island of Sri Lanka, the river basins of southeast Asia, the mountain monasteries of China, Korea, and Japan, and the hermitages of the Himalayan kingdoms. But the last lap of its journey is without parallel. Today Buddhist meditation has been lifted from its traditional setting in Buddhist doctrine and faith and transplanted in a secularized culture bent on pragmatic results. Here it is finding new accommodations in urban meditation centers and even in busy hospitals, pain clinics, and treatment centers. Its teachers and practitioners are more likely to wear street clothing or white coats than ochre robes; they are more likely to hold degrees in medicine and psychology than in Buddhist philosophy and scripture. Meditation is being taught to help people obtain release, not from the cycle of birth and death, but from the strains of financial pressures, psychological disorders, and stressful relationships.

---

92. The four types of clear comprehension are discussed at length in Nyanaponika 1962: 45–55. I have translated the commentarial explanation in Bodhi 2008: 94–130.

As stress-reduction specialists and psychotherapists seek new methods to help their patients deal with physical pain, grief, and distress, the ancient system of mindfulness meditation offers fresh promise. But the response from the Buddhist side has not been exclusively enthusiastic. Confirmed adherents of Buddhism have given the secular adaptation of Buddhist meditation mixed reviews. While some applaud the application of mindfulness to an array of new fields, from medical centers to high schools to maximum security prisons, others have reacted with skepticism if not with shrill denunciations. Many sincere Buddhists, still undecided, struggle with questions to which the canonical texts provide no clear answers: "Is the pure Dhamma being diluted for secular ends, reduced to a mere therapy? Won't the outcome be to make saṃsāra more pleasant rather than to liberate people from the cycle of rebirths? Did anyone ever attain enlightenment in a medical clinic?"

It's my personal belief that we need to strike a balance between caution and appreciation. There is a real danger that scientists who investigate traditional eastern contemplative practices might be swayed by materialistic premises to explain their efficacy reductively, on the exclusive basis of neurophysiology. There is a real danger that the contemplative challenge might be reduced to a matter of gaining skill in certain techniques, dispensing with such qualities as faith, aspiration, devotion, and self-surrender, all integral to the act of "going for refuge." However, I don't think we need be alarmed about the adaptation of Buddhist practices for secular ends. I call to mind a statement the Buddha made in the weeks before his death: "The Tathāgata has no closed fist of a teacher with respect to teachings."[93] By this he meant that he had taught everything important without holding back any esoteric doctrines, but I like to interpret his words to mean that we can let anyone take from the Dhamma anything they find useful even if it is for secular purposes.

I feel that if psychotherapists can draw upon Buddhist mindfulness practice to help people overcome anxiety and distress, their work is most commendable. If clinicians find that mindfulness helps patients accept pain and illness, that is wonderful—and having a chronic pain condition myself, I give extra kudos to their work. If peace activists find the meditation on loving-kindness helps them be

93. DN 16.2.25 (D II 100; LDB 245).

more peaceful in their advocacy of peace, again, that is splendid. And if a businessman finds his Zen practice makes him more considerate of his clients, again this should merit our approval.

It's inevitable that mindfulness and other practices adopted from Buddhism will find new applications in the modern West, where worldviews and lifestyles are so different from those of southern and eastern Asia. If such practices benefit those who don't accept the full framework of Buddhist teaching, I see no reason to grudge them the right to take what they need. To the contrary, I feel that those who adapt the Dhamma to these new purposes are to be admired for their pioneering courage and insight. As long as they act with prudence and a compassionate intent, let them make use of the Dhamma in any way they can to help others.

At the same time, I also believe that it's our responsibility, as heirs of the Dhamma, to remind such experimenters that they have entered a sanctuary deemed sacred by Buddhists. Thus, respectful towards their sources, they should pursue their investigations with humility and gratitude. They should recognize that while the Dhamma bids everyone come and take what they need, they are drawing from an ancient well of sacred wisdom that has nourished countless spirits through the centuries and whose waters still retain their potency for those who drink from them today.

# BIBLIOGRAPHY

Bodhi, Bhikkhu, translator. 2000. *The Connected Discourses of the Buddha: A Translation of the Saṃyutta Nikāya*, Boston: Wisdom Publications.

Bodhi, Bhikkhu, translator. 1989, reprint 2008. *The Fruits of Recluseship: The Sāmaññaphala Sutta and its Commentaries*, Kandy, Sri Lanka: Buddhist Publication Society.

Bodhi, Bhikkhu, translator. 2012. *The Numerical Discourses of the Buddha: A Translation of the Aṅguttara Nikāya*, Boston: Wisdom Publications.

Fronsdal, Gil. 1995. "Treasures of the Theravada: Recovering the Riches of Our Tradition." Originally published in *Inquiring Mind*, Vol 12(1). Available at: www.insightmeditationcenter.org.

Gunaratana, Henepola. 2002. *Mindfulness in Plain English*, Boston: Wisdom Publications.

Mahasi Sayadaw. 1971, reprint 2006. *Practical Insight Meditation*, Kandy, Sri Lanka: Buddhist Publication Society.

Monier-Williams, Monier. reprint 2005. *Sanskrit-English Dictionary*, Delhi: Motilal Banarsidass.

Ñāṇamoli, Bhikkhu and Bhikkhu Bodhi, translators. 1995. *The Middle Length Discourses of the Buddha: A Translation of the Majjhima Nikāya*, Boston: Wisdom Publications.

Ñāṇamoli, Bhikkhu, translator. 1964. *The Path of Purification (Visuddhimagga)*. Reprint 1991, Kandy, Sri Lanka: Buddhist Publication Society.

Nyanaponika Thera. 1962. *The Heart of Buddhist Meditation*, London: Riders. Reprint 1992, Kandy, Sri Lanka: Buddhist Publication Society.

Nyanaponika Thera. 1968, reprint 2014. *The Power of Mindfulness*, Kandy, Sri Lanka: Buddhist Publication Society.

Rhys Davids, T.W. and C.A.F., translators. 1910. *Dialogues of the Buddha*, London: Pali Text Society.

Walshe, Maurice, translator. 1995. *The Long Discourses of the Buddha: A Translation of the Dīgha Nikāya*, Boston: Wisdom Publication.

# Deconstructing Constructions: The Role of *Saṅkhārā* in the Buddha's Discourses

## 1. Introduction

In this paper I intend to explore the Pāli term *saṅkhārā*, one of the pivotal concepts in the Buddha's discourses. The Pāli word has such a rich gamut of meanings that merely to draw them out into the open sheds a flood of light on the Buddha's understanding of reality. The word occurs in a variety of contexts that are subtly and intricately interwoven. To explore their contextual meanings and track down their interconnections will reveal the rigor of the Buddha's philosophical vision and the coherence of his teaching in expressing that vision in language and concepts.

The noun *saṅkhārā* (a plural form) is derived from the prefix *saṃ-*, which suggests "together" (like the English prefix "con-" or "com-"), joined to the noun *kārā*, meaning "deeds, acts." Etymologically, *saṅkhārā* are thus "co-doings." The corresponding verb, *saṅkharoti*, derived from the prefix *saṃ-* and the verb *karoti*, "to make, to do," can mean "to construct, to put together, to compose." Both the noun and the verb are sometimes augmented by another prefix, *abhi-*, to yield a substantive noun *abhisaṅkhāra*, an action noun *abhisaṅkharaṇa* (found only in the commentarial literature), and a verb *abhisaṅkharoti*. The addition of the prefix *abhi-* usually suggests the involvement of conscious agency in the act of doing or making. This, however, is not invariably the case and the word *abhisaṅkhāra* is found in instances when no conscious agency is involved.[94]

---

94. One such instance is in a statement describing the motion of a wheel, at A I 111–12, *taṃ pavattitaṃ samānaṃ yāvatikā abhisaṅkhārassa*

As we will see, the word *saṅkhārā* has both an active sense and a passive sense. This means that *saṅkhārā* are at once things that act in unison with other things to produce effects and the things produced by the combined efficacy of those causal forces. Translators of Pāli into English have rendered the word in a variety of ways: formations, confections, activities, processes, fabrications, forces, compounds, compositions, concoctions, determinations, synergies, constructions. All such renderings are clumsy attempts to capture the meaning of a concept for which Western thought has no exact parallel.

However, though it may be impossible to discover an exact English equivalent for *saṅkhārā*, by exploring its usage in the texts we can see how the word functions in the "thought world" of the Buddha's teachings. In this paper I will focus primarily on the place of the *saṅkhārā* in the suttas, the discourses of the Buddha. On occasion, however, I will turn to the commentaries for clarification of the primary texts.

In the suttas we can distinguish *four major doctrinal contexts* in which the concept of *saṅkhārā* plays a major role. I will first explore these contexts individually. Then I will look at them in conjunction to see how a synoptic view of the *saṅkhārā* can help us understand the Buddha's understanding of actuality. Finally, I will relate these meanings to the end goal of the Buddha's teaching, the realization of nibbāna, liberation from *dukkha*.

## 2. SAṄKHĀRĀ IN DEPENDENT ORIGINATION

One context where the word *saṅkhārā* frequently occurs is in the twelve-fold formula of dependent origination (*paṭicca-samuppāda*). Here, *saṅkhārā* is the second link in the series, conditioned by ignorance (*avijjāpaccayā saṅkhārā*) and serving as the condition for consciousness (*saṅkhārapaccayā viññāṇaṃ*). In the discourses, the relationship between these three terms is usually expressed simply by this abstract formula, without the conceptual elaboration we would expect from a modern account of Buddhist doctrine. It is likely that the Buddha explained these relationships in greater detail,

---

*gati tāvatikaṃ gantvā*, where *abhisaṅkhāra* corresponds to the notion of "momentum."

but when the compilers collected the texts, they may have reduced the diverse and more complex explanations to this terse formula as an aid to memorization and oral transmission.

Several suttas, however, analyze the *saṅkhārā* and thus shed light on the role they play in the process of dependent origination. Such texts "slice up" the *saṅkhārā* in two complementary ways. One analysis distinguishes them by way of the "doors of action," the other by way of their ethical tone. Distinguished through door of action, the *saṅkhārā* become threefold:

> "And what, monks, are the volitional activities? There are these three kinds of volitional activities: the bodily volitional activity, the verbal volitional activity, the mental volitional activity. These are called the volitional activities."[95]

The *Sāratthappakāsinī*, the commentary to the Saṃyutta Nikāya, explains *saṅkhāra* in this context as the act of "volitionally constructing" (*abhisaṅkharaṇalakkhaṇo saṅkhāro*). It goes on to define the bodily volitional activity as the wholesome and unwholesome bodily volitions (*kāyasañcetanā*) that instigate action through the door of body; the verbal volitional activity as the wholesome and unwholesome verbal volitions (*vacīsañcetanā*) that instigate action through the door of speech; and the mental volitional activity as mundane wholesome and unwholesome mental volition (*manosañcetanā*) that occurs solely in the mind, without instigating action through body and speech.[96]

In this role, the word *saṅkhārā* is virtually synonymous with *kamma*, a word to which it is etymologically akin, both being derived from the verb *karoti*, "to act, to do, to make." *Saṅkhārā* may thus be understood as the inner volitional activity that creates kamma, deeds with the potential to produce results corresponding

---

95. SN 12:2/S II 4: *Katame ca, bhikkhave, saṅkhārā? Tayome, bhikkhave, saṅkhārā—kāyasaṅkhāro, vacīsaṅkhāro, cittasaṅkhāro. Ime vuccanti, bhikkhave, saṅkhārā*. In the context of dependent origination, I use "volitional activities" as a provisional rendering for *saṅkhārā*. But as will be clear, no rendering of this word into English fully succeeds in capturing the interconnection between the nuances it takes on in its different contexts.

96. Spk II 17. The explanation relates these volitions to the states of consciousness (*citta*) in the Abhidhamma system as delineated in the Dhammasaṅgaṇī, but this degree of detail is not relevant to our inquiry.

to their own moral quality. The connection between the two is reinforced by the well-known passage in which the Buddha says: "It is volition, monks, that I call kamma. For having willed (that is, exercised volition), one acts by body, speech, and mind."[97]

The second scheme used to distinguish the *saṅkhārā* in dependent origination is based on their ethical quality. This analysis is again threefold, as indicated by a text that not only lays down this threefold classification but illuminates the inter-relationship between the three types of *saṅkhārā*, their condition, ignorance (*avijjā*), and their fruit, consciousness (*viññāṇa*):

> "Monks, if a person immersed in ignorance constructs a meritorious volitional activity, consciousness fares on to the meritorious. If he constructs a demeritorious volitional activity, consciousness fares on to the demeritorious. If he constructs an imperturbable volitional activity, consciousness fares on to the imperturbable."[98]

The commentary explains meritorious volitional activity (*puññaṃ saṅkhāraṃ*) as the volition comprised in sense-sphere wholesome states of consciousness and the form-sphere wholesome volition of the jhānas. Demeritorious volitional activity (*apuññaṃ saṅkhāraṃ*) is the volition involved in unwholesome states of consciousness, and imperturbable volitional activity (*āneñjaṃ saṅkhāraṃ*) the volition involved in the formless attainments.

Of interest here is the verb *abhisaṅkharoti*, which characterizes the activity of the "person immersed in ignorance" (*avijjāgata*), and the suffix-*upaga*, which characterizes the fate of consciousness under the influence of the *saṅkhārā*. The verb *abhisaṅkharoti* suggests that through the act of volition a person "constructs" a particular kind of volitional activity, meritorious, demeritorious, or imperturbable, which manifests through body, speech, or mind. It is noteworthy that ignorance underlies *all such volitional activity*,

97. AN 6:63/A III 415: *Cetanā'haṃ, bhikkhave, kammaṃ vadāmi. Cetayitvā kammaṃ karoti kāyena vācāya manasā.*

98. SN 12:51/A II 82: *Avijjāgato yaṃ, bhikkhave, purisapuggalo puññaṃ ce saṅkhāraṃ abhisaṅkharoti, puññūpagaṃ hoti viññāṇaṃ. Apuññaṃ ce saṅkhāraṃ abhisaṅkharoti, apuññūpagaṃ hoti viññāṇaṃ. Āneñjaṃ ce saṅkhāraṃ abhisaṅkharoti āneñjūpagaṃ hoti viññāṇaṃ.*

even that classified as meritorious and imperturbable. This reveals ignorance as the root of all activity pertaining to the "round of birth and death," whether conventionally considered good or bad. Even wholesome deeds, when pursued for the sake of some karmic benefit, and even the imperturbable meditations, when underlaid by a subtle clinging, create a karmic potential that keeps one in bondage to the cycle of rebirths.

The volitional activity generates a kamma, which in turn eventually bears fruit. The principal fruit of kamma may be conceived as the "construction" of a new state of existence in a realm appropriate to the generative kamma. But the *saṅkhārā* will also yield their particular fruits in the course of a lifetime. Using another metaphor, we might say that the volition infuses the state of consciousness with its own ethical quality—either meritorious, demeritorious, or imperturbable—and the consciousness so infused is then propelled to a new state of existence that corresponds to its ethical quality.

We meet the suffix *-upaga* in another formula often occurring in the Nikāyas, which helps to illuminate its meaning in the passage under consideration. This other formula describes one of the higher knowledges accessible to the Buddha and the arahants, the knowledge of the passing away and rebirth of beings (*sattānaṃ cutūpapātañāṇa*). In describing his own attainment of enlightenment (at MN 4/M I 22), the Buddha says: "With the divine eye, purified and surpassing the human, I saw beings passing away and being reborn, inferior and superior, beautiful and ugly, fortunate and unfortunate. I understood how beings fare on according to their kamma (*yathākammūpage satte pajānāmi*)." In this description -*upaga* signifies that beings "fare on" to the destination that accords with their kamma. Those who commit unwholesome deeds of body, speech, and mind move on toward the miserable destinations of rebirth. Those who do wholesome deeds move on toward the fortunate destinations of rebirth.

The same principle should apply to SN 12:51. In explicating this passage, the Saṃyutta Commentary says that the volitional activity influences both kinds of consciousness, the karmically generative consciousness and the resultant consciousness.[99] Thus

99. Spk II 78: *Puññūpagaṃ hoti viññāṇan ti kammaviññāṇaṃ kamma-puññena upagataṃ sampayuttaṃ hoti, vipākaviññāṇaṃ vipākapuññena.*

when one performs a meritorious deed, the meritorious volitional activity moves the consciousness associated with itself toward merit, imbuing consciousness with its own meritorious character. And so for the other two types of volitional activity.

But this does not mark the end of the impact the volitional activities have on consciousness. Propped up by ignorance and fueled by craving, the *saṅkhārā* drive the stream of consciousness onward to a new birth, and exactly where consciousness winds up is determined by the ethical character of the *saṅkhārā*. If one engages in meritorious deeds, the *saṅkhārā* will propel consciousness toward a fortunate sphere of rebirth. If one engages in demeritorious deeds, the *saṅkhārā* will propel consciousness toward rebirth in a lower realm. And if one masters the formless meditations, the imperturbable *saṅkhārā* will propel consciousness toward rebirth in the formless realm.

## 3. SAṄKHĀRĀ AS THE FOURTH AGGREGATE

A second major sphere to which the word *saṅkhārā* applies is the five aggregates, the fourth of which is the *saṅkhārakkhandha*. This we may render as "the aggregate of volitional activities." The texts explicitly define the *saṅkhārakkhandha* as the six classes of volition:

> "And what, monks, are volitional activities? There are these six classes of volition: volition regarding forms, volition regarding sounds, volition regarding odours, volition regarding tastes, volition regarding tactile objects, volition regarding mental phenomena. These are called volitional activities."[100]

Though these *saṅkhārā* correspond closely to those in the formula of dependent origination, the two may not be identical in all respects. This is certainly the case according to the Abhidhamma and its commentaries, which consider the *saṅkhārakkhandha* to be classifiable as karmically unwholesome, karmically wholesome, resultant, and merely functional. From this perspective, it is only the karmically unwholesome and wholesome volitions that are included in the second factor in the chain of dependent origination.

---

100. SN 22:56/S III 60: *Katame ca, bhikkhave, saṅkhārā? Chayime, bhikkhave, cetanākāyā—rūpasañcetanā, saddasañcetanā, gandhasañcetanā, rasasañcetanā, phoṭṭhabbasañcetanā, dhammasañcetanā. Ime vuccanti, bhikkhave, saṅkhārā.*

Although this position is not explicitly stated in the suttas, it may be justified in the light of certain passages that show the *saṅkhārakkhandha* to be integral to all experience. As a universal constituent of experience, the *saṅkhārakkhandha* must encompass *all kinds of volition*, not only those that generate kamma. Since volition, or *cetanā*, is one of the invariable factors in *nāma*, "name" or "mentality," a term that represents the factors present on any occasion of cognition, the *saṅkhārakkhandha* must be present even on occasions of experience that are passive or inert in terms of their karmic potential. While the idea of "resultant volition" (*vipākacetanā*), found in the Abhidhamma commentaries, is not mentioned in the Nikāyas, implicit support for the idea of karmically neutral *saṅkhārā* may be provided by the Mahāhatthipadopama Sutta (MN 28), spoken by Venerable Sāriputta. In the second half of this sutta, after Sāriputta has expounded on the four material elements, he goes on to explain how, in the genesis of any experience, all five aggregates come to be. In regard to visual experience the exposition is as follows (M I 190):

> "When internally the eye is intact and external forms come into its range, and there is the corresponding mental engagement, then there is manifestation of the corresponding section of consciousness. The form in what has thus come to be is included in the form aggregate subject to clinging. The feeling in what has thus come to be is included in the feeling aggregate subject to clinging. The perception in what has thus come to be is included in the perception aggregate subject to clinging. *The volitional activities in what has thus come to be are included in the volitional activities aggregate subject to clinging.* The consciousness in what has thus come to be is included in the consciousness aggregate subject to clinging."

Since the occasion being described is one when consciousness passively cognizes a visible form that has just entered the range of perception, we may assume that a response decisive enough to create kamma has not yet occurred. However, since the text speaks of the *saṅkhārakkhandha* as already present, we might take the volitional activity on this occasion to be a type of response that operates at a pre-karmic level, perhaps as the rudimentary volition involved in the bare cognitive reception of the sense object. If we were to use the taxonomy of the Abhidhamma system, according to which eye-consciousness (and the other types of sensory consciousness) is a resultant consciousness, we would call this a resultant type of volitional activity. As resultant, it would have to be excluded from the *saṅkhārā* factor of dependent origination, and yet as a type of volition, it would be comprised by the *saṅkhārakkhandha*.

Nevertheless, since the Buddha's teaching is not concerned with a purely objective analysis of experience for its own value, but with understanding how we create *dukkha* or suffering, his focus would have been on the more active dimensions of the *saṅkhārakkhandha*, especially as the engine that shapes the interpretation of cognitive events and drives the production of kamma. We will return to this aspect of the *saṅkhārakkhandha* below.

In the later Pāli literature, beginning perhaps with the Dhammasaṅgaṇī, the *saṅkhārakkhandha* serves as an umbrella category to which all mental factors can be assigned, with the exception of feeling and perception, which are aggregates in their own right. Thus the *saṅkhārakkhandha* is considered to include such ethically variable factors as thought, attention, mental unification, joy, and effort; such wholesome factors as non-greed, non-hatred, moral shame, moral dread, compassion, mindfulness, and wisdom; and such unwholesome factors as greed, hatred, and delusion. Since all these factors arise in conjunction with volition, the early Buddhist teachers must have decided that the most fitting place to assign them is in the aggregate of volitional activities. While the suttas do not expressly assign these other factors to a place among the five aggregates, the ancient teachers must have felt that if the scheme of the aggregates is truly all-inclusive, a place must be found for the undetermined mental factors, and the fourth aggregate seemed the best candidate for this role.

## 4. Saṅkhārā as All Conditioned Things

The third sphere in which the notion of *saṅkhārā* plays a major role is indicated by the expression *sabbe saṅkhārā*, a designation for *all* conditioned things. According to the Pāli commentaries, in this context the word denotes whatever is produced by conditions: whatever is conditioned, constructed, or fabricated. The commentaries designate these *saṅkhārā* as *saṅkhatasaṅkhārā*,

"*saṅkhārā* consisting in the conditioned," *saṅkhata* being the past participle of the verb *saṅkharoti* from which the noun *saṅkhārā* is derived. Thus the Abhidhamma commentary *Sammohavinodanī* (p. 135) states that "all phenomena accompanied by conditions are '*saṅkhārā* consisting in the conditioned' (*sabbepi sappaccayā dhammā 'saṅkhatasaṅkhārā' nāma*)." In this sense the word might be rendered simply as "conditioned phenomena." A subset of this category, according to the same passage of the *Sammohavinodanī*, consists of the material and mental phenomena of the three planes of existence specifically produced by kamma; these, it says, are called in the ancient commentaries "*saṅkhārā* consisting in the *volitionally* conditioned" (*kammanibbattā tebhūmakā rūpārūpadhammā 'abhisaṅkhatasaṅkhārā'ti aṭṭhakathāsu vuttā*), that is, conditioned phenomena that are partly constructed by the activity of volition.

This derivation would give the word *saṅkhārā* an essentially passive connotation. However, to view the *saṅkhārā*, taken in this most comprehensive sense, as inherently passive may impose on the term too constrictive a meaning. As an alternative, we might see *saṅkhārā* in this broad sense as functioning simultaneously in two roles, as both active conditions and as the conditioned phenomena constructed and sustained by conditions. Support for this perspective might be gleaned from at least two passages in the suttas. One supportive text is SN 48:40/S V 213–15, which discusses the five faculties connected with feeling and the stages where they "cease without remainder" (*aparisesaṃ nirujjhati*). Here, the Buddha declares with respect to each of these faculties: *tañca kho sanimittaṃ sanidānaṃ sasaṅkhāraṃ sappaccayaṃ*. We might render this phrase: "and that is with a basis, with an origin, with constructive activity, with a condition."[101]Thus the word *saṅkhāra*, in what appears to be a situation where volitional activity is not necessarily involved, is collated with three other words that denote causation: *nimitta*, *nidāna*, and *paccaya*, each qualified by the prefix *sa-*, meaning "along with, together with." Since the conditions or constructive activities

101.For instance, with regard to the faculty of pain (*dukkhindriya*), it is said at S IV 213: *Uppannaṃ kho me idaṃ dukkhindriyaṃ, tañca kho sanimittaṃ sanidānaṃ sasaṅkhāraṃ sappaccayaṃ*. The commentary, Spk III 241, explains: "All these words, *nimitta* and the others, are simply synonyms for condition" (*nimittantiādīni sabbāni paccayavevacanān'eva*).

productive of feeling could be the impact of the object, the acuity of the sense faculty, the act of attention, and so forth, we need not see the volitions of the *saṅkhārakkhandha* as intended here.

The other passage is a series of short suttas (at A I 82), in which it is said that bad unwholesome qualities (*pāpakā akusalā dhammā*) arise *sanimittā sanidānā sahetukā sasaṅkhārā sappaccayā*, "with a basis, with an origin, with a cause, with constructive activity, with a condition." The sequence of terms, it will be noted, is identical with that in SN 48:40, but with the addition of *hetuka*, derived from *hetu*, meaning "cause." Again, this indicates that *saṅkhārā*, in the broad sense, can be considered as also exercising an active function that is not necessarily tied to volition.

On such an interpretation, which ascribes both causal activity and passivity to them, the *saṅkhārā* in the comprehensive sense could be regarded as nodes in a complex network of conditioning factors. Within this network, each node, each *saṅkhāra*, is connected to the others in a variety of ways. Each *saṅkhāra*, as conditioned, points backward to the cluster of past conditions from which it originates, but as an active condition it also points forward to the future phenomena it helps to produce and laterally to the cluster of present phenomena it helps to sustain.

As conditioned phenomena, *saṅkhārā* include *all five aggregates*, not just the fourth aggregate. Thus, for instance, when the debater Saccaka asks the Buddha how he trains disciples, the Buddha replies: "Form is impermanent, feeling is impermanent, perception is impermanent, volitional activities (*saṅkhārā*) are impermanent, consciousness is impermanent.... All *saṅkhārā* are impermanent."[102]The same idea is enunciated in verses 277–78 of the Dhammapada:

"All conditioned phenomena are impermanent" ...
"All conditioned phenomena are suffering":
when one sees this with wisdom,
one becomes disenchanted with suffering.
This is the path to purity.

---

102. MN 35/M I 230: "*Rūpaṃ, bhikkhave, aniccaṃ, vedanā aniccā, saññā aniccā, saṅkhārā aniccā, viññāṇaṃ aniccaṃ.... Sabbe saṅkhārā aniccā.*" This instruction is also given to the monk Channa at SN 22:90/S III 132.

As these verses imply, the *saṅkhārā* serve as the epitome of *dukkha*, the first noble truth, encapsulating in one word its deeper meaning. When the Buddha summarizes the first noble truth by declaring, "In brief, the five aggregates subject to clinging are *dukkha*," he brings all conditioned phenomena into the range of *dukkha*. And all such phenomena are *dukkha* precisely because they are produced by conditions.

In the Nikāyas, we encounter a threefold analysis of *dukkha*: *dukkha* entailed by suffering, *dukkha* intrinsic to conditioned phenomena, and *dukkha* entailed by change.[103] The *Sumaṅgalavilāsinī*, the Dīgha Nikāya Commentary (at III 992), identifies the first as painful feeling, which is inherently suffering, and the third as pleasant feeling, which is unsatisfactory because subject to change. It identifies the second, *saṅkhāradukkhatā*, with neutral feeling, feeling that is neither painful nor pleasant, on the ground that such feeling is oppressed by arising, decay, and dissolution (*uppādajarābhaṅgapīḷitā*). The commentary adds, however, that because of the statement "all *saṅkhārā* are *dukkha*," all phenomena of the three realms of existence, apart from painful and pleasant feeling (which fall under their own respective types of *dukkha*), are comprised in "the *dukkha* intrinsic to conditioned phenomena." This way of distributing the three feelings among the three types of *dukkha* may still be too narrow and even contrary to the Nikāyas. The Buddha himself says that when he declared, "Whatever is felt is included in *dukkha*," he declared this with reference to the impermanence of the *saṅkhārā*.[104] Thus on the authority of this statement, all three types of feeling can be included in *saṅkhāradukkhatā*, the "suffering intrinsic to conditioned phenomena."

It is with reference to *saṅkhārā* in this sense that the Buddha issues his familiar exhortation to attain release from the cycle of rebirths (for instance, at SN 15:1/S II 178):

---

103. *Dukkhadukkhatā, saṅkhāradukkhatā, vipariṇāmadukkhatā*. This triad is at D III 216, S IV 259, and S V 56. See too *Visuddhimagga* 499; Ch. XVI.34–35.

104. SN 36:11/S IV 216: *Vuttaṃ kho pan'etaṃ, bhikkhu, mayā 'yaṃ kiñci vedayitaṃ, taṃ dukkhasmin'ti, taṃ kho pan'etaṃ, bhikkhu, mayā saṅkhārānaṃyeva aniccataṃ sandhāya bhāsitaṃ.*

> "Monks, this saṃsāra is without discoverable beginning. A first point is not discerned of beings roaming and wandering on hindered by ignorance and fettered by craving. For such a long time, monks, you have experienced suffering, anguish, and disaster, and swelled the cemetery. It is enough, monks, to be disenchanted with all *saṅkhārā*, enough to be dispassionate towards them, enough to be liberated from them (*yāvañc'idaṃ, bhikkhave, alameva sabbasaṅkhāresu nibbindituṃ alaṃ virajjituṃ alaṃ vimuccituṃ*)."

Since the wandering in saṃsāra is maintained by ignorance and craving, the path to liberation, the path that will "deconstruct" the constructing and constructed phenomena of the *saṅkhārā*, devolves upon the task of eliminating ignorance and craving. This requires vigorous effort, and thus in his last exhortation (at D II 156 and S I 157) the Buddha again stressed the same point: "*Saṅkhārā* are subject to vanish. Achieve the goal by heedfulness" (*vayadhammā saṅkhārā appamādena sampādetha*).

## 5. THE SEQUENTIAL CESSATION OF SAṄKHĀRĀ

A fourth domain to which the word *saṅkhārā* applies is the stages of meditation. The term *saṅkhārā* here refers to certain factors that are to be gradually stilled as one progresses through the successive levels of meditative attainment. We find this usage in the Ānāpānasati Sutta (MN 118), where the first tetrad speaks about "pacifying the bodily activity" (*passambhayaṃ kāyasaṅkhāraṃ*) and the second tetrad about "pacifying the mental activity" (*passambhayaṃ cittasaṅkhāraṃ*). But the fullest treatment of this group of *saṅkhārā* is the Cūḷavedalla Sutta (MN 44),[105] which takes the form of a dialogue between the nun Dhammadinnā and the layman Visākha. Here, the bodily *saṅkhāra* (a grammatical singular) is identified with inhalation and exhalation, "because these things are bodily, dependent on the body." The verbal *saṅkhāra* is identified with thought and examination, "because first one thinks and examines, and then breaks out into speech." And the mental *saṅkhāra* is identified with

105. At M I 301. There is a parallel passage at SN 41:6/S IV 293, which takes the form of a conversation between the monk Kāmabhū and the layman Citta the Householder.

perception and feeling, "because these things are mental, dependent on the mind." In the development of deeper meditative states, the verbal *saṅkhāra* ceases with the attainment of the second jhāna, in which thought and examination subside; the bodily *saṅkhāra* ceases with the attainment of the fourth jhāna, in which breathing stops; and the mental *saṅkhāra* ceases with "the attainment of the cessation of perception and feeling."

This scheme, which relates *saṅkhārā* to the progressive stages of meditation, is subsumed under the project of bringing certain *saṅkhārā* to an end, both tentatively in higher meditative attainments and permanently through wisdom. In the sutta in which the Buddha designates all three types of feeling as *dukkha* because of their impermanence, he goes on to introduce what he calls "a sequential cessation of *saṅkhārā*" (*anupubbasaṅkhārānaṃ nirodha*).[106] Thus for one who enters the first jhāna, speech has ceased; for one who attains the second jhāna, thought and examination (*vitakkavicārā*) have ceased; and so, in each of the attainments beyond this, successively more subtle factors cease until one attains "the cessation of perception and feeling" (*saññāvedayitanirodha*), when perception and feeling (and all other mental activities) cease.

But even this attainment does not mark the end of the sequence, for such cessation is only temporary. Beyond even this exalted meditative state, the sutta says, lies the attainment of arahantship. It is in the arahant that "lust has ceased, hatred has ceased, and delusion has ceased" (*khīṇāsavassa bhikkhuno rāgo niruddho hoti, doso niruddho hoti, moho niruddho hoti*). Thus lust, hatred, and delusion are here depicted as the most stubborn *saṅkhārā* of all, those particular phenomena, at once constructing and constructed, that drive the process of becoming. And the goal of the spiritual life is held up as the cessation of lust, hatred, and delusion, fully achieved only by the arahant.

---

106. SN 36:11/S IV 217. See too AN 9:31/A IV 409, where, however, what ceases in the first jhāna is sensual perception rather than speech. In the same extended passage this is also called a sequential stilling of *saṅkhārā* (*anupubbasaṅkhārānaṃ vūpasama*). Six kinds of subsiding (*passaddhi*) are also mentioned here, the stilling of the coarser factors pertaining to the four jhānas, the stilling of perception and feeling in the attainment of cessation, and the stilling of lust, hatred, and delusion in the arahant.

## 6. A Synoptic Perspective on the Saṅkhārā

The fact that *saṅkhārā* can include both active forces and the things produced by them secures for the term a role as the cornerstone of the Buddha's philosophical vision. What the Buddha teaches is that the *saṅkhārā* in the two active senses—the volitional activities operative in dependent origination, and the karmically creative volitional activities in the fourth aggregate—construct *saṅkhārā* as the volitionally produced conditioned phenomena comprised in the five aggregates. These latter can also be expressed as the particular personhood (*attabhāva*) we acquire as we take up one existence after another in the round of birth and death.

This role of the *saṅkhārā* can be illustrated by two passages, one pertaining to *saṅkhārā* as the second factor of dependent origination, the other to *saṅkhārā* as the fourth among the five aggregates. The passage I have in mind pertaining to dependent origination, however, does not employ the standard twelve-fold formula but a unique variant. The use of such variants demonstrates that the terms in the familiar twelve-term series should not be seen as locked into a fixed and invariable sequence but as participants in a complex process that can be viewed from a variety of angles. This particular sutta (SN 12:64; II 101–3) begins with the "four nutriments" (*cattāro āhārā*): material food, contact, mental volition, and consciousness. It continues thus:

> "If there is lust, delight, and craving [for any of the four nutriments], consciousness is established there and comes to growth. Wherever consciousness is established and comes to growth, there is a descent of name-and-form. Where there is a descent of name-and-form, there is the growth of *saṅkhārā*. Where there is the growth of *saṅkhārā*, there is production of future renewed existence. Where there is production of future renewed existence, there is future birth, old age, and death. Where there is future birth, old age, and death, that, I say, is accompanied by sorrow, anguish, and despair."

In this passage, the *saṅkhārā* follow upon consciousness and name-and-form rather than preceding them as in the standard formula. We can thus infer that these are the volitional activities that occur *after* a new life has begun, that is, after craving has propelled the stream of consciousness into a new existence, which like any existence consists in the interplay of consciousness and name-and-form. But once the new life starts and consciousness and name-and-form begin to weave around each other, fresh volitional activities emerge, "constructing" still another existence in the future, a life that begins with birth and continues into old age and death. The sutta illustrates the "constructive" role of the volitional activities in shaping the new existence with the fitting simile of artistic creation:

> "Suppose an artist, using paint of different colors, would create the figure of a man or a woman complete in all its features on a well-polished plank or wall or canvas. So too, if there is lust and craving [for any of the four nutriments], consciousness is established there and comes to growth.... that, I say, is accompanied by sorrow, anguish, and despair."

The second passage I wish to consider is found in the Khajjaniya Sutta (SN 22:79), a discourse that attempts to explain the functions of each of the five aggregates. Here, the Buddha assigns to the *saṅkhārakkhandha* a constructive role in relation to all five aggregates. The relevant passage (at S III 87) relies on a convergence of word forms that is notoriously hard to replicate in translation. The text begins by raising the question, "Why does one call them *saṅkhārā*?" The answer given, in Pāli, is: *saṅkhatam abhisaṅkharontīti kho, bhikkhave, tasmā 'saṅkhārā'ti vuccati.* To capture the subtle word play in this answer, I will render *saṅkhārā* by the clumsy expression "constructive volitional activities." The reason they are called "constructive volitional activities" might then be translated: "They volitionally construct the constructed, monks, therefore they are called constructive volitional activities." The text next asks, "What is the constructed that they volitionally construct (*kiñca saṅkhatam abhisaṅkharonti*)?" And in reply it asserts:

> "They volitionally construct constructed form in accordance with the nature of form (*rūpaṃ rūpattāya saṅkhatam abhisaṅkharonti*);[107] they volitionally construct constructed

107. The commentary (Spk II 292) explains this rather obscure expression thus: "As one makes porridge in accordance with the nature of porridge and bakes a cake in accordance with the nature of cake, so one constructs, assembles, amasses, produces that volitionally constructed thing called 'form'—which

feeling in accordance with the nature of feeling; they volitionally construct constructed perception in accordance with the nature of perception; they volitionally construct constructed volitional constructions in accordance with the nature of volitional constructions; they volitionally construct constructed consciousness in accordance with the nature of consciousness. They volitionally construct the constructed, therefore they are called constructive volitional activities."

Though external inanimate objects may arise from purely physical causes, from the evidence of this passage we can infer that the *saṅkhārā* that make up our personal being—the five aggregates—are all products of the karmically active *saṅkhārā* generated in our previous lives as well as those being fashioned in our present life. Thus, the Buddha teaches, it was our own karmically constructive *saṅkhārā* that have built up our present edifice of personal being, and it is our present constructive *saṅkhārā* that are building up the edifices of personal being we will inhabit in future lives. These "edifices" consist of nothing other than the *saṅkhārā* as the conditioned phenomena comprised in the five aggregates. These go on conditioning each other throughout our present life, and via the *saṅkhārā* of the fourth aggregate, build up still more edifices of being in future lives, until they are finally disabled or "deconstructed."

## 7. DECONSTRUCTING CONSTRUCTIONS

The most important fact to understand about *saṅkhārā*, as conditioned phenomena, is that they are all impermanent. As stated in the famous verse recited at Buddhist funerals: "Impermanent, alas, are conditioned things" (*aniccā vata saṅkhārā*). They are impermanent not only in the sense that in their gross manifestations they will eventually cease to be, but even more pointedly because at the subtle level they constantly undergo rise and fall. Forever they

---

is conditioned because it is made by the convergence of such conditions—in accordance with its nature as form, so that it gets to be called form." (*Rūpaṃ rūpattāya saṅkhatamabhisaṅkharontīti yathā yāgumeva yāguttāya, pūvameva pūvattāya pacati nāma, evaṃ paccayehi samāgantvā katabhāvena saṅkhatanti laddhanāmaṃ rūpameva rūpattāya yathā abhisaṅkhataṃ rūpaṃ nāma hoti, tathattāya rūpabhāvāya abhisaṅkharoti āyūhati sampiṇḍeti, nipphādetīti attho.*)

are coming into being and then breaking up and perishing; hence "their very nature is to arise and vanish" (*uppādavayadhammino*). For this reason the Buddha declares that all *saṅkhārā* are suffering (*sabbe saṅkhārā dukkha*)—suffering, however, not because they are all actually painful and stressful, but because they are stamped with the mark of transience. "Having arisen they then cease" (*uppajjitvā nirujjhanti*), and because they all cease they cannot provide stable happiness and security.

To win complete release from *dukkha* one must attain release not only from experiential suffering but from the unsatisfactoriness intrinsic to all conditioned existence. This is the aspect of *dukkha* highlighted by the expression *saṅkhāradukkha*, the dimension of suffering inseparable from conditioned phenomena. What lies beyond the *saṅkhārā* is that which is *asaṅkhata*, unconditioned, not constructed, not put together, not compounded by saṅkhārā. And that which is not compounded by saṅkhārā is nibbāna. Nibbāna is designated the unconditioned precisely because it is a state that is neither itself a saṅkhāra nor one constructed by saṅkhārā. It is a state reached when, as stated in Dhammapada verse 154, all craving is destroyed and the mind reaches the deconstruction, the deactivation, the disabling, of constructive activities (*visaṅkhāragataṃ cittaṃ taṇhānam khayaṃ ajjhagā*).

Nibbāna is also designated *sabbasaṅkhārasamatha*, "the stilling of all conditioned phenomena." How this "stilling" is accomplished is described in the sutta referred to earlier, at SN 12:51/S II 82. After the Buddha has classified the *saṅkhārā* of dependent origination by way of their ethical quality, he goes on to explain how a monk stops constructing *saṅkhārā* and thereby reaches nibbāna:

> "But when a monk has abandoned ignorance and aroused true knowledge, then, with the fading away of ignorance and the arising of true knowledge, he does not construct a meritorious volitional activity, or a demeritorious volitional activity, or an imperturbable volitional activity (*n'eva puññābhisaṅkhāraṃ abhisaṅkharoti na apuññābhisaṅkhāraṃ abhisaṅkharoti na āneñjābhisaṅkhāraṃ abhisaṅkharoti*). Since he does not construct or fashion volitions (*anabhisaṅkharonto anabhisañcetayanto*), he does not cling to anything in the world. Not clinging, he is not agitated. Not being agitated, he personally attains nibbāna. He

understands: 'Destroyed is birth, the holy life has been lived, what had to be done has been done, there is no more for this state of being.'"

This passage indicates that the *saṅkhārā* are to be finally deconstructed, not by suppression, not by a forceful attempt to destroy them, but by arousing true knowledge (*vijjā*). And as we learn from many other texts, true knowledge arises through the practice of the noble eightfold path or the sequential training in virtuous conduct, concentration, and wisdom. When such knowledge arises, it eliminates the ignorance and craving that underlie the process of karmic activity and thereby brings to an end both the constructing activity of present *saṅkhārā* and the construction of future *saṅkhārā*. This liberates one from bondage to the round of births, so that one comes no more to "this state of being" (*itthattāya*), to any state of "this-ness" in the three realms of existence.

Thus, when we put the word *saṅkhārā* under the microscope, we can see compressed within it the entire worldview of the Dhamma. The active *saṅkhārā* consisting in karmically active volitions perpetuate the *saṅkhārā* of the five aggregates that constitute a sentient being. We identify with the five aggregates because of ignorance, and we seek enjoyment in them because of craving. On account of ignorance and craving, we engage in volitional activities that build up future combinations of the five aggregates, which in total are all *saṅkhārā*, and these become our personal identities in successive lives. Just that is the nature of *saṃsāra:* an unbroken procession of empty but efficient *saṅkhārā* producing still other *saṅkhārā*, rising up in fresh waves with each new birth, swelling to a crest, and then crashing down into old age, illness, and death. Yet on it goes, shrouded in the delusion that we're really in control, sustained by an ever-tantalizing, ever-receding hope of final satisfaction.

When, however, we take up the practice of the Dhamma, we apply a brake to this relentless generation of *saṅkhārā*. Through wisdom we remove ignorance; through renunciation we remove craving. We see with wisdom the true nature of the *saṅkhārā*, of our own five aggregates, as unstable, conditioned processes rolling on with no essential persisting self in charge. Thereby we switch off the engine driven by ignorance and craving, and the process of karmic construction, the production of active *saṅkhārā*, is effectively shut down. By putting an end to the constructing of conditioned reality, we open the door to what is ever-present but not constructed, not conditioned: the *asaṅkhata-dhātu*, the unconditioned element. This is nibbāna, the deathless, the subsiding of constructive volitional activities, final liberation from all conditionings and thus from impermanence and death. Therefore the popular verse concludes: "The subsiding of *saṅkhārā* is blissful (*tesaṃ vūpasamo sukho*)."

# ABOUT PARIYATTI

Pariyatti is dedicated to providing affordable access to authentic teachings of the Buddha about the Dhamma theory (*pariyatti*) and practice (*paṭipatti*) of Vipassana meditation. A 501(c)(3) nonprofit charitable organization since 2002, Pariyatti is sustained by contributions from individuals who appreciate and want to share the incalculable value of the Dhamma teachings. We invite you to visit www.pariyatti.org to learn about our programs, services, and ways to support publishing and other undertakings.

## Pariyatti Publishing Imprints

***Vipassana Research Publications*** (focus on Vipassana as taught by S.N. Goenka in the tradition of Sayagyi U Ba Khin)

***BPS Pariyatti Editions*** (selected titles from the Buddhist Publication Society, copublished by Pariyatti in the Americas)

***Pariyatti Digital Editions*** (audio and video titles, including discourses)

***Pariyatti Press*** (classic titles returned to print and inspirational writing by contemporary authors)

## Pariyatti enriches the world by

- disseminating the words of the Buddha,
- providing sustenance for the seeker's journey,
- illuminating the meditator's path.